MW01621988

THE HIDDEN WORLDS

The Visionary Art of Gilbert Williams, Volume II

Visionary Publishing, Inc.
302 South County Road, Suite 230
Palm Beach, FL 33480, 407/697-7771

Works by Gilbert Williams

Books

Illuminations: The Visionary Art of Gilbert Williams (Volume I), a book of 40 color plates with an Introduction by Peny North

The Hidden Worlds: The Visionary Art of Gilbert Williams, Volume II, a book of 36 color plates with an Introduction by Jach Pursel and Gilbert Williams

Original Paintings & Lithographs

Available exclusively from Isis Rising, The Galleria at Fort Lauderdale (next to Neiman Marcus), 2398(A) East Sunrise Boulevard, Unit E-15, Fort Lauderdale, Florida 33304, 305/566-8088

Notecards, Books, and the annual *Lazaris - Gilbert Williams Calendar*

Available from Visionary Publishing, Inc., 302 South County Road, Suite 230, Palm Beach, FL 33480, 407/697-7771

(Please see back page of book for further information.)

THE HIDDEN WORLDS

An original publication by Visionary Publishing, Inc.
302 South County Road, Suite 230
Palm Beach, Florida 33480, 407/697-7771

Introduction by Jach Pursel and Gilbert Williams
Book design by Peny North

Printed in the United States of America

INTRODUCTION

A Conversation with Jach Pursel and Gilbert Williams ...

August, 1989

Jach: Starting at the beginning ... When did you first realize you wanted to paint and draw?

Gilbert: Let's see ... I've been painting and drawing all my life, since I can remember. When I was five I was always drawing. I would just go through reams of paper sometimes, just drawing things all the time.

Jach: Do you know why? Can you remember back? Why was it so important to you?

Gilbert: It was fun. I think it was a positive escape. You know, I just had so many things in my head — in my imagination. I wanted to get them out, and somehow I think they wanted to get out, too. I would go to museums — I loved to do that — I would go to museums and see the art. I would just stand there and stare. It was really fascinating to me. It stimulated me.

I wanted to do that. I wanted to take all these pictures inside my head and put them on paper. I wanted to see them outside of me as well as inside of me. I wanted to be able to put the pictures out in front of me and just look at them — like I did in the museum.

Jach: What kind of pieces did you first draw?

Gilbert: A lot of science fiction things — rocket ships, robots, and fantasy things like that. Like most kids, I was fascinated by futuristic and prehistoric things. I was fascinated by dinosaurs and by all those things of the "scientific world" inside a kid's head. So I started drawing those things in a sort of fantastic way.

Jach: Do you still have any of those things? Do you still have any of your childhood drawings?

Gilbert: I don't personally, no.

Jach: You don't?

Gilbert: My mother may ... who knows?

Jach: Do you remember if those early drawings had the surreal quality that your work has now?

Gilbert: They were drawings of my imagination. I don't think they had a particular style. I wasn't so interested in drawing pictures for their own sake. I wasn't trying to make a statement or anything. I wasn't interested in drawing the things that were around me so much. I wanted to get the images out of my head and onto the paper so I could see them, so I could play in that world more easily.

No, I don't think they were surreal. They were just me. You know, I didn't set something up to paint. I wasn't trying to reproduce something that was real.

Most people learn to paint by setting up the things they want to include in the painting. They try to copy — they try to reproduce what is tangibly there. They work to develop a style or an expression.

Not me. I just wanted to bring the fantasy in my head into the reality of my bedroom. So, no, I doubt that they were surreal or that they represented any style for that matter.

Jach: So you never did do still life paintings with flowers and things?

Gilbert: Well, I did some still life, not flowers and things, mainly faces and things. But I would just make them up out of my imagination. No one posed for me, that's for sure.

Jach: Do you think you always knew from the time you were very small that you'd be an artist, or did you ever have sort of something in your mind like, "OK, I'm going to be a doctor," or whatever?

Gilbert: At one point I seriously thought I might be a scientist. I now realize that my mind isn't structured that way. ... {Laughter} ... But I was always skilled at art. At school, they would always pull my drawings and, by that time, put my paintings in the art shows. I got a lot of encouragement for that. I gained a lot of skill just from the encouragement, I think. I know I gained a great deal of motivation from it.

Jach: So it was all self-taught at that point, then?

Gilbert: Oh, yeah. As I look back now, I never thought about my art as an occupation so much as a thing I had to do as part of my self-expression. I always had a drawing board set up somewhere, or an easel.

Jach: When did your work move away from the "scientific thing" into the more magical and visionary quality it now has? I know your work is always evolving, but when did the visionary quality begin? When did it start happening?

Gilbert: Probably back in the early '60s. Pictures of angels, and other Symbolist-type images, showed up in my mind and subsequently came out in my work.

I would just sit down with a blank sheet of paper, and these images would just manifest themselves. I mean, I would draw them, but they would almost seem to be coming out of the paper just as I was drawing them on the paper. It intrigued me no end.

I started getting a little interested in metaphysics at that time, too. You know, I studied a little Hinduism and Zen. I read some Alan Watts. That sort of thing, not heavy. So it sort of crept into my consciousness there.

I was also in a period of a lot of self-examination. I was still a teenager when all this happened.

As we all do from time to time, and as teenagers do a lot, I was looking at the meaning of life ... {laughter} ... but while I was looking, it seemed that there was a point — a point about life — that everybody around me was missing.

I almost became obsessive about trying to find out what that "something missing" was. I wanted to know why we exist and all that. Now I realize everyone goes through all that, but then I thought I was the only one who knew "something was missing."

I had to find the answer. People all around me were living shallow lives in a sterile world. I was living in Southern California at the time. ... {laughter} ... There were a lot of very uptight and conservative people who lived all around me. They seemed just very short-sighted. It just seemed to me that there had to be a whole lot more depth in the world out there somewhere. I was missing it.

There was no nature around me. At that point in my life, there were some big pieces missing. I tried to find it in my painting.

Jach: OK, so a new kind of imagery shows up in your work. You are beginning the first steps of a mental and philosophical search to find something meaningful. And that's when work took on much more of the visionary quality that it has now?

Gilbert: Right.

Jach: At some point you must have gone from always having that drawing table and sketch pad set up, because it was so absolutely necessary for your self-expression, to realizing that you were going to be a painter for the rest of your life. When did that happen?

Gilbert: Probably when I was living up in Mt. Shasta. I think it all crystallized up there. My style just came through. All the pieces fit together. Suddenly I had a style that was mine. I had a style that I liked and a style that seemed to express what I wanted to say.

Also, I found technical instruments like an airbrush and a more effective understanding of color ... a few things like that.

It all fell together along with my philosophy at that point. I knew what I wanted to paint.

At that time, I started doing some paintings just for myself. I had a job painting little pictures on leather garments ... {laughter} ... just to make money. So I started painting paintings for myself. And everybody seemed to really like them. I put them up in a local store, and people really responded to my work. I was surprised and very happy. And the people responding were not just the people coming up to Mt. Shasta looking for Lemurians living in the mountains, either ... {laughter} ... so I took them down to the Bay Area. First came notecards. Then my originals began to sell. The feedback was wonderful. That's how it all began.

Jach: It seems like what you're saying is that the philosophy and art came together all at once. At that point in your life, they kind of crossed paths really ... and you realized this is what I'm going to do in this lifetime. Avocational or vocational, this is what you were going to do.

Gilbert: Yes. I got in touch with a certain part of my soul, I think, and it was not so much because of the philosophy everybody was spouting around there. No, it wasn't the particulars of the philosophy at all. It's just that I started having experiences up there that were definitely metaphysical experiences. They overshadowed my cynical/critical mind. They were more real than my cynical/critical mind. And I could not deny the realness of those experiences.

I was seeing people's auras and all sorts of things. Also, I would fall into this elevated state of consciousness from meditating. You know, just being around people who were into metaphysics all their life ... I'd get stuff from them that was really other worldly. There were some people there who really had very powerful emanations, even though I didn't particularly agree with everything they said or believed. They were very powerful and impactful.

Jach: They put out a resonance ...

Gilbert: You have to understand that at that time, even though I was interested in metaphysics, I had not seen a lot of proof, and a lot of it seemed like fairy tales. Now it is different for me. Metaphysics is real — very real — to me now. But then it was different. But while I was there, I had some experiences with people where they actually ... just being with them ... my consciousness raised almost involuntarily. It was sort of what people call the *shakti* thing.

Jach: There's a question that I have to ask about the whole creative process for you. When you start to paint a painting, is it already a full picture in your mind, or does it unfold as you go? Does a painting stay the same in your mind and on canvas from beginning to end, or does it change?

Gilbert: It changes. Sometimes I'll start with a very vivid image, and I'll try to paint it, and by the time I'm halfway done, it's actually mutated.

It's like a dream changes as I paint. It's very fluid like that. The whole composition could change, turn from a day scene to a night scene, for example. It's very fluid, and if I try to structure it to really try to reproduce the initial vision, I'll lose that initial vision eventually. Unless I'm doing a real small painting where I could do it real fast, I'll usually lose it — and if I try to force it, it'll get like really stilted. That's where I lose the quality sometimes, so I have to trash the whole thing sometimes. But if I let it flow, it's a lot of fun.

Jach: Have you ever been really surprised? Like you started to paint something, and what came out was different and surprising to you?

Gilbert: Yeah, sort of. It's an ongoing process. It doesn't really happen suddenly, but things do really change a lot ... winds up being something totally different from what I started to do.

Jach: I've heard a number of people talk about the creative process, and some of them have said that when they get involved in it, for a while they are doing it, and then it seems to be doing itself. Simultaneously, the very process is doing something to them as well. Do you think that that's true for you?

Gilbert: Definitely.

Jach: Then we get to the real bottom-line question: What is it like to paint this imagery?

Gilbert: It's like dreaming in a really funny way, because the process of painting is coming from one fraction of myself. It's like almost ... oh, I know, when I see one of my paintings that I haven't seen in a very long time, it's as if someone else did the painting. I often won't even recognize my own paintings because it's like it's this one part of my mind that's doing it.

Jach: So when you're actually in the process it is like a dream unfolding ...

Gilbert: Yeah, it has its own reality and its own depth. It's almost like a photograph that's out of focus and slowly comes into focus. So I'm using a process where I'm layering layers on layers on layers, and as that happens often things will change unexpectedly, and then it'll turn into something else. And its very much like the way dreams will mutate.

Jach: That's fascinating. Now to another bottom line: What does it do to you, for you? What does it give you when you paint the painting? What do you get from it? Obviously, there are commercial aspects, but what do you get from the actual piece?

Gilbert: It's hard to put it into words. I get a certain sense of satisfaction when it works very smoothly, and it's an almost indescribable feeling.

It's not just the feeling of feeling real great because I did something good. It's a feeling of being unblocked ... it's like if you're playing music and everything just flows, and it's unblocked, and it's perfect. It's like a release of energy that otherwise would feel very frustrated, and it's like ... boy ... it's just like a sense of satisfaction in my soul that I can't even describe. When I paint, that's what I feel — that's what it gives me.

Jach: It's not just a physical satisfaction ... you are talking about something much deeper than that ... it's a soul level.

Gilbert: There's something in the creative level and the soul level that is really satisfied when everything just kind of falls into place and it works just right.

Jach: ... What makes Visionary Art visionary art? ... Why does it have such impact on people?

Gilbert: On one level, I think all good art is Visionary Art. What sets what we call Visionary Art apart ... it's hard to put into words, it's ... the aim of it, I suppose ... every kind of art in a way is representational. Every kind of art is representational.

It's like an illustration. Even an abstract painting is an illustration — is a representation of something.

And I think Visionary Art is an illustration of the spiritual imagination. When you're thinking in the resonance of spirituality, it sets up images of a certain resonance, I think. And that's what I think Visionary Art is. It is the representation — the illustration — of spiritual imagination.

And so if I'm truly in my spiritual imagination when I'm creating, I think other people resonate to that. Also, it stimulates images in their own mind that may not even be on the canvas.

Jach: What it sounds like you're saying is that by your being in a certain place — in a certain resonance — when you're painting where you are representing your spiritual imagination, not only the image but also that resonance goes onto the canvas. Then when people view the painting, they see not only the image, but they pick up the resonance. Is that correct?

Gilbert: Right. I think it stimulates everybody else's spiritual imagination. You see, everyone is just as loaded with images as I am. I am able to express it on canvas, that's all.

I'll get letters from people, and they will write about a particular painting and what it meant to them. They will often have this whole array of images that pours out of their minds. The painting sets that off.

Jach: That's why ... why I know you don't really want to explain to people what your paintings mean.

Gilbert: I really think it's an important part of this experience for people to dream their own dreams as they are viewing my work.

Jach: What roles do archetypal images play in Visionary work and in your work?

Gilbert: I think there are certain images that express the soul's hunger, that express the soul's hunger for meaning, for evolution. That's why certain images are called archetypal in the first place. The soul wants to be wiser. There are certain images like a wise man or a wise woman that keep cropping up. It's a part of my spiritual imagination. It's a part of each of our spiritual imaginations. The hunger is in each of us.

Jach: A great deal of what you do you have taught yourself. What about formal training? Have you taken classes?

Gilbert: Yes, I've taken lots of classes over the years. When I was twelve years old I started taking oil painting classes. When I got into college, I didn't go for a degree. I went to learn something. I had a couple of really good drawing teachers here and there, but mostly I learned from reading books about technique and about materials.

Jach: You spent a lot of time learning about the nature of pigment. You really have studied that quite a lot.

Gilbert: I never really had to go to school for that because I found it a lot easier just to go through the books and absorb it all.

Jach: What did that give you, do you think, learning about how they made pigments and about the history of pigments?

Gilbert: I think it put me in touch with a lot of the tradition of art. I think that is very important. As I stretch out there, you know, into the spiritual imagination, the tradition — the tradition of art — becomes very important, not important so much as grounding as it is as appreciation.

When I was a little kid spending all that time at the museums staring at those old paintings, I had almost a psychic feeling for what the people back then were thinking when they were painting. When you're in the presence of the original art, there's a feeling — something really special. It's sort of spooky in a special way. It's like some sort of psychometrizing, I suppose. Anyway, I ... feel something very amazing when I open up with oil paintings. So I am fascinated with the whole history of art.

It really hooked me. The tradition of painting and painters is very important to me. In my way, I want to capture a piece of that tradition in my visionary paintings and in the visionary-abstract work that I am doing now. There's something really subtle about the dreamlike state of, say, the pre-Raphaelite paintings, for example. I really can't put it into words.

Jach: Well, thank you for the words you did use. Now, a final topic: Your work is being reproduced by Visionary Publishing, Inc., as notecards and calendars. There are going to be several other methods of making your work available to people. How do you feel about doing a calendar every year, these books, and all the other things you and Peny *(Peny North, CEO of Visionary Publishing, Inc., and of Isis Rising, Inc., the exclusive agent for Gilbert Williams' work)* have been designing?

Gilbert: I think the reproductions are great, because they get the work out in a form that's accessible to lots of people. I am really pleased when a work sells to a private collector, but it is also sad to know that work will be seen only by a few people — the friends of the collector. Reproductions are wonderful.

The calendar is great because each month you live with the painting for a little while ... as you're daydreaming you may look at it, and it may set off a whole set of things that are totally unaffiliated with the painting.

It's a wonderful way to start a dream. So I think the calendar is really wonderful because you can daydream with it. Often when you're in a situation with an office ... well, you can imagine.

The books work the same way, but when you have more time, when you can be more leisurely in your pursuit. I am glad to have these two books out. I look forward to the next.

Jach: You could even use the book as something of an *I Ching* ...

Gilbert: Uh-huh. Visionary Art is really meant to be sort of a reflection of the viewer as much as it is an expression for the artist. ...

CONTENTS

The Plates

1. Ascending Stones
2. Dance of the Nature Spirits
3. Elemental Dance
4. Faces of the Goddess
5. Far Vistas
6. Fountain of Renewal
7. Invocation
8. Jeweled Path
9. Night Forest
10. The Path
11. Portal
12. Portal of the Pleiades
13. Reflection Pool
14. Sacred Forest
15. The Shrine
16. Treasure Ship
17. Visualization
18. Wisdom
19. Abundance
20. Cloud Spirit
21. Crystal Fountain
22. Dolphin Dawn
23. Entrance into the Earth
24. Explorers
25. Far Horizons
26. The Gathering
27. Gathering Flowers
28. Hidden Worlds
29. Illumination Window
30. Homeward Travelers
31. Lady of the Lake
32. Lazaris Remembers Lemuria
33. Mist Angel
34. Sacred Journey
35. Troubadour of Spring
36. The Way Shower

1. ASCENDING STONES

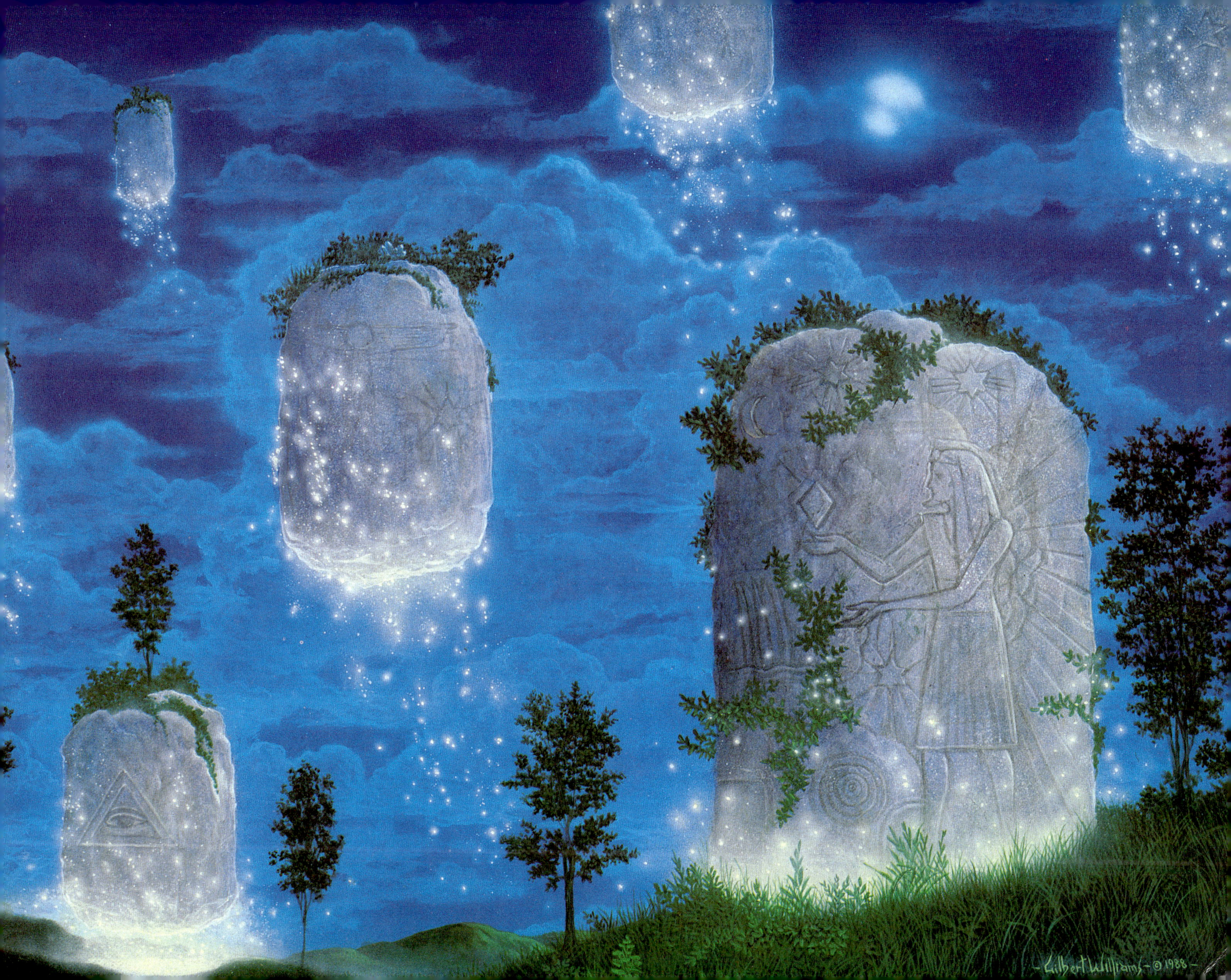
- Gilbert Williams - © 1988 -

2. DANCE OF THE NATURE SPIRITS

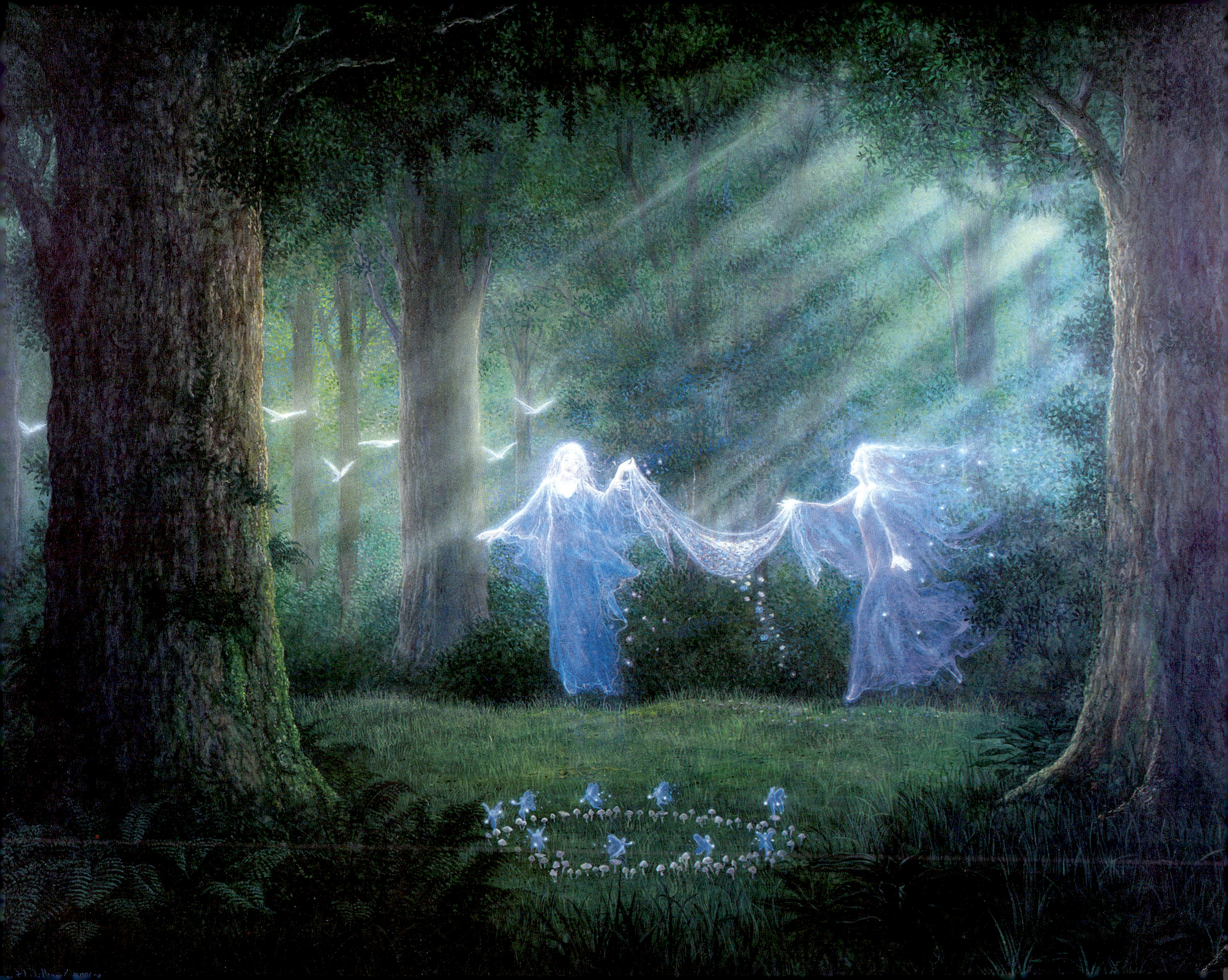

3. ELEMENTAL DANCE

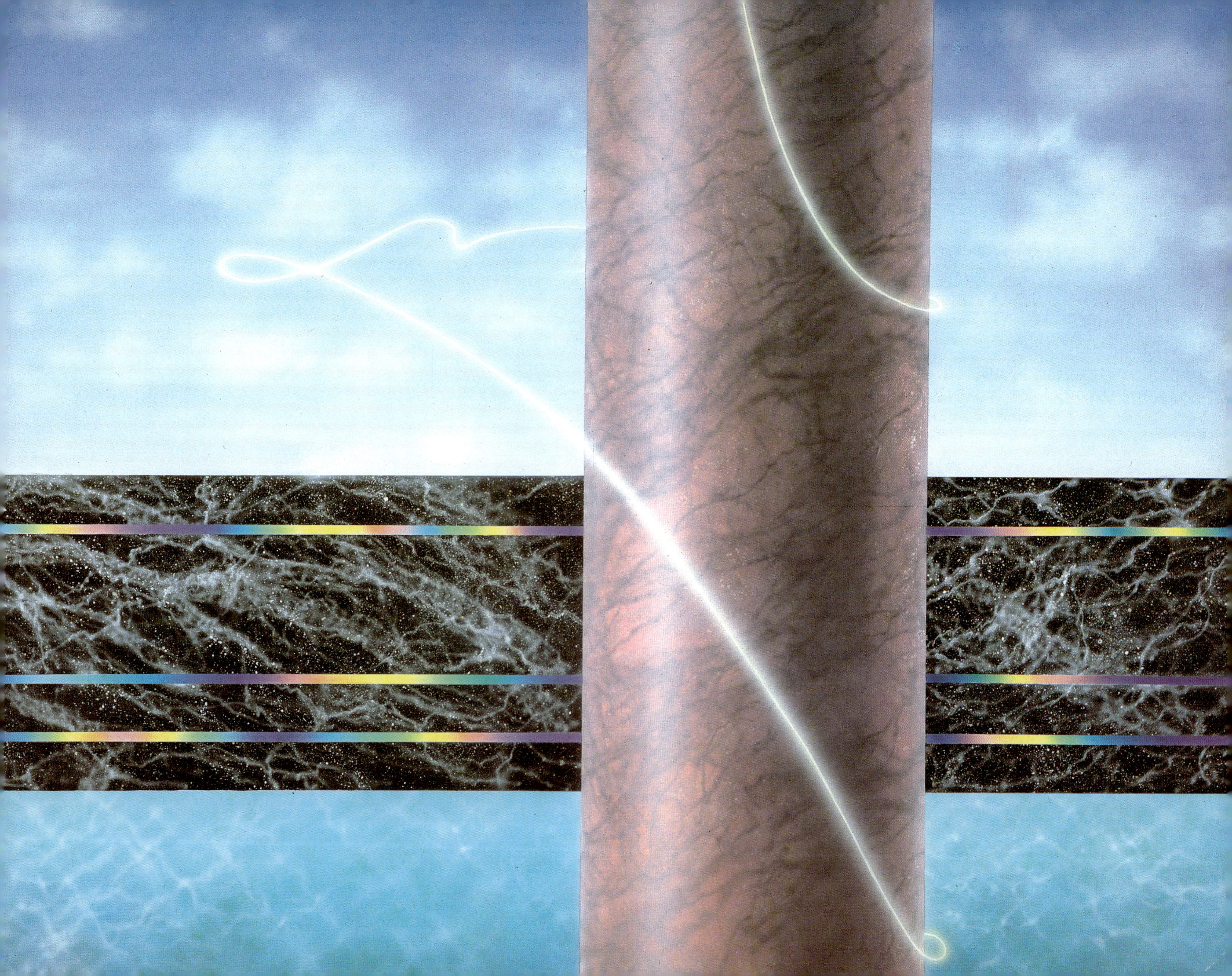

4. FACES OF THE GODDESS

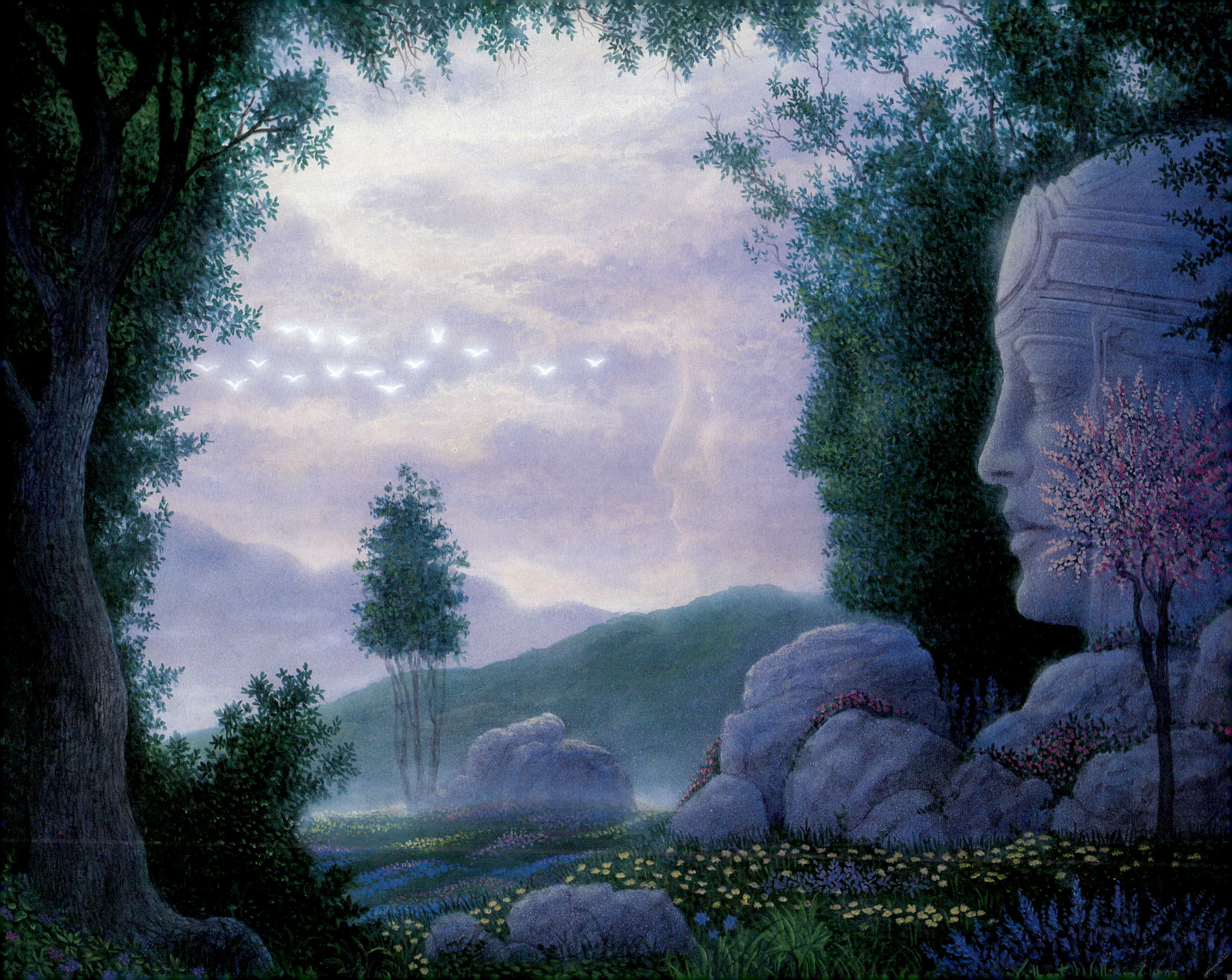

5. FAR VISTAS

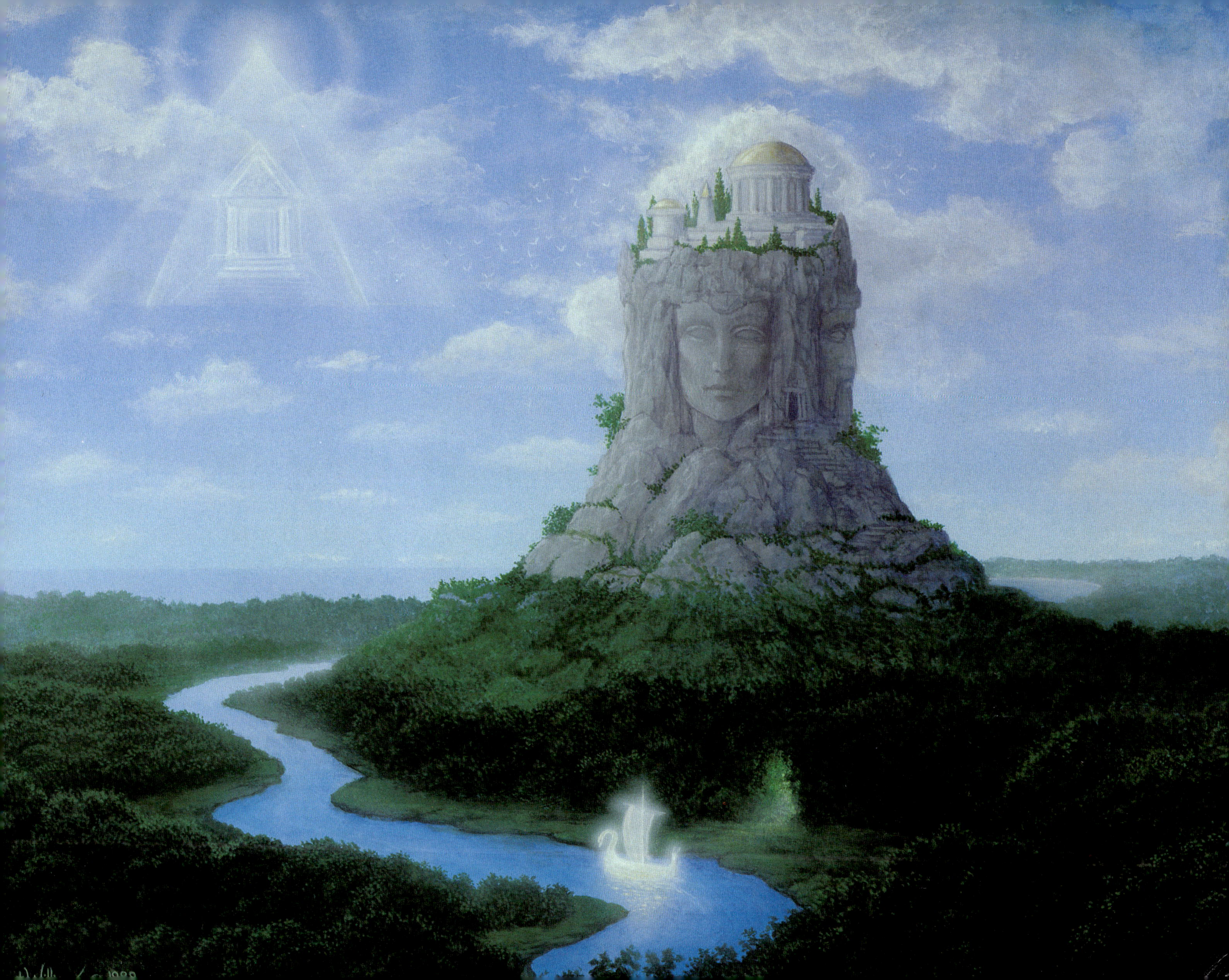

6. FOUNTAIN OF RENEWAL

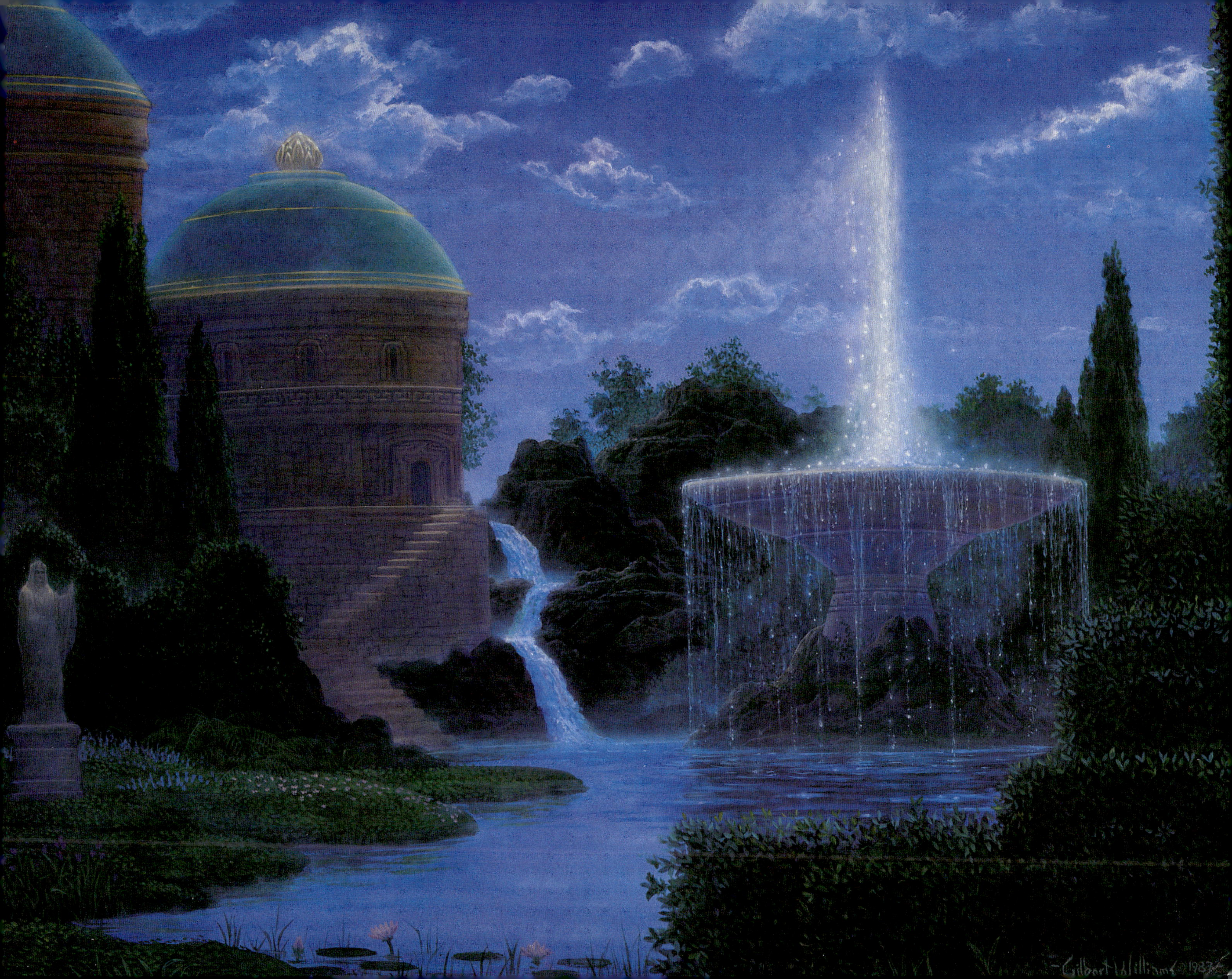
Gilbert Williams

7. INVOCATION

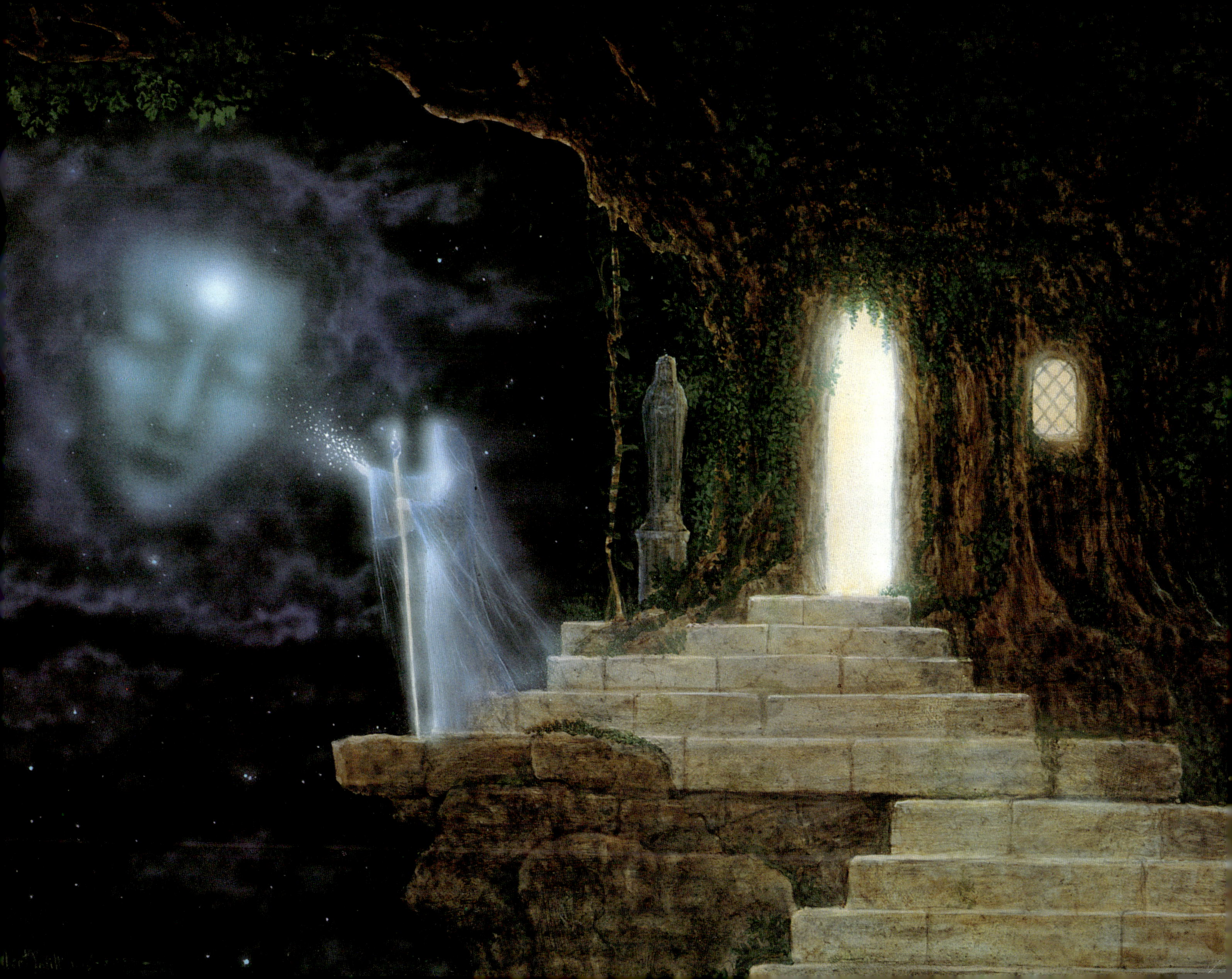

8. JEWELED PATH

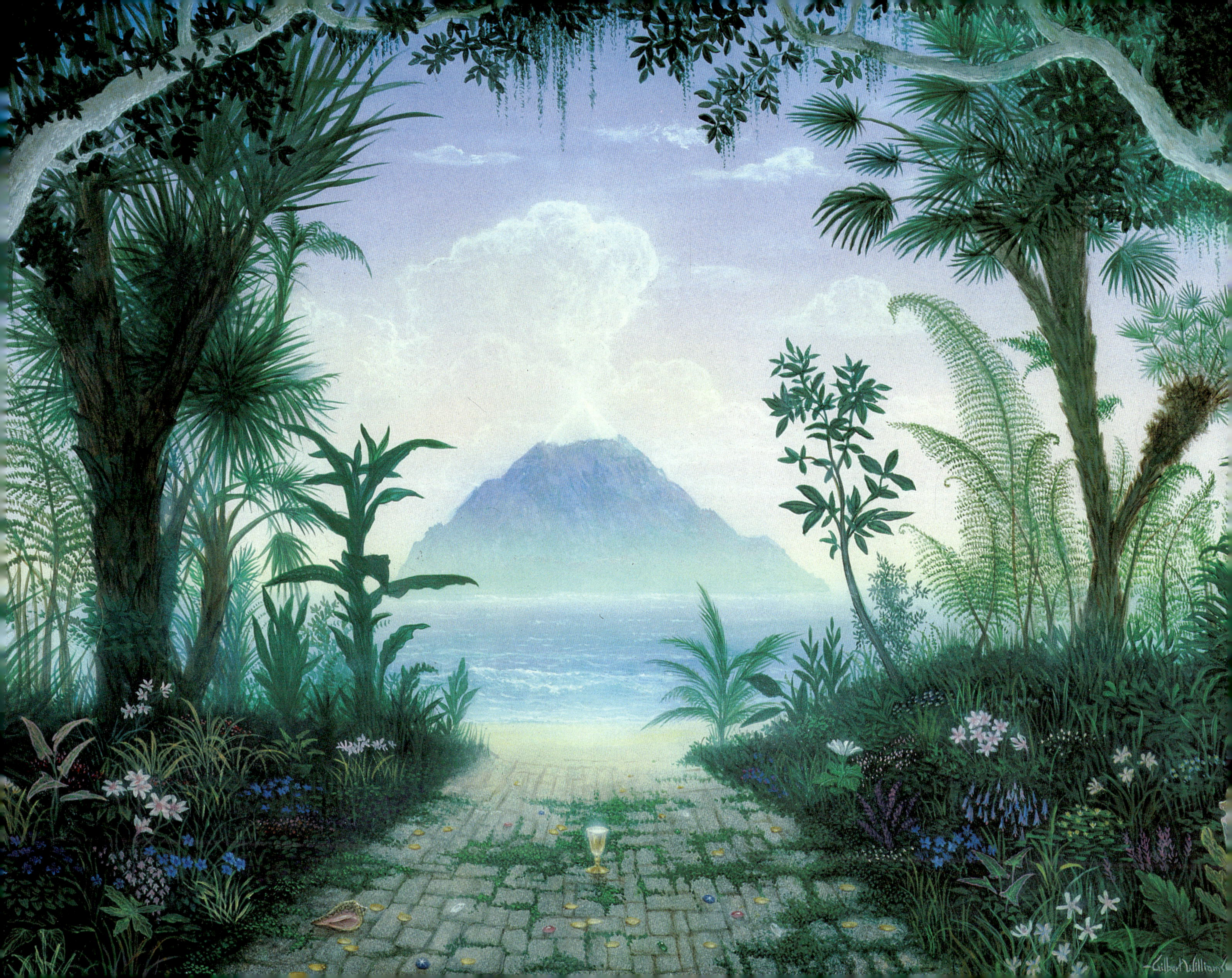
Gilbert Williams

9. NIGHT FOREST

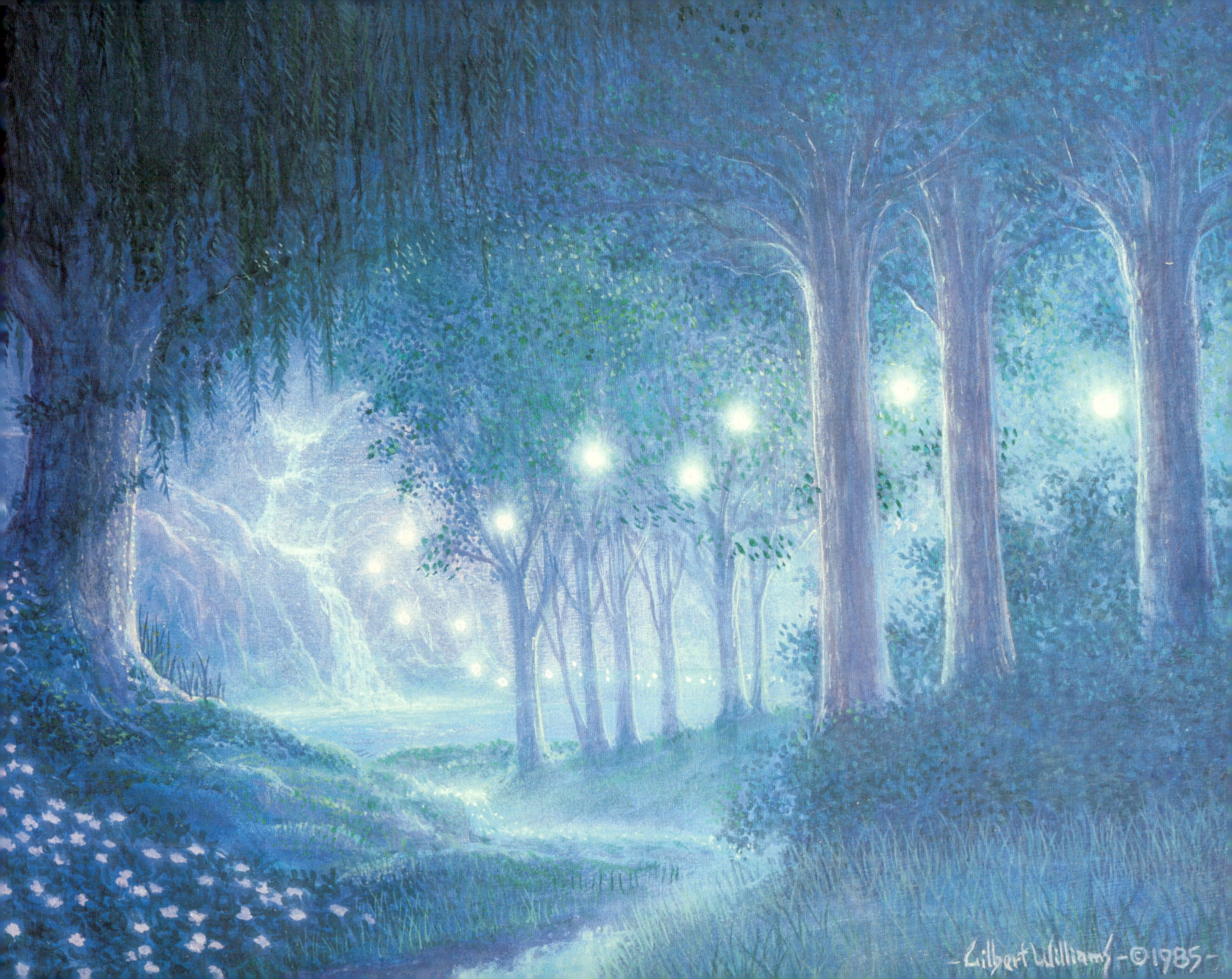
-Gilbert Williams-©1985-

10. THE PATH

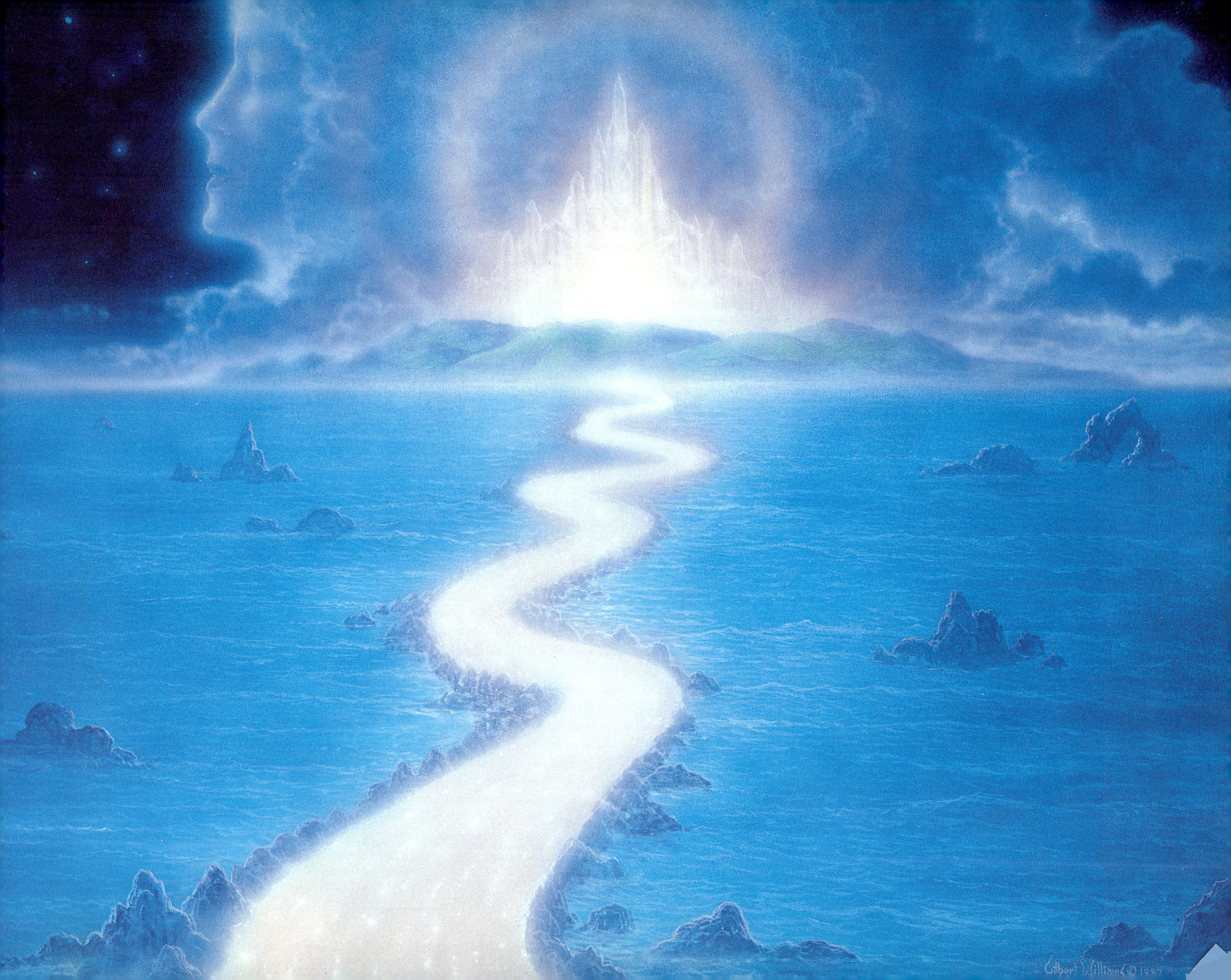
Gilbert Williams ©

11. PORTAL

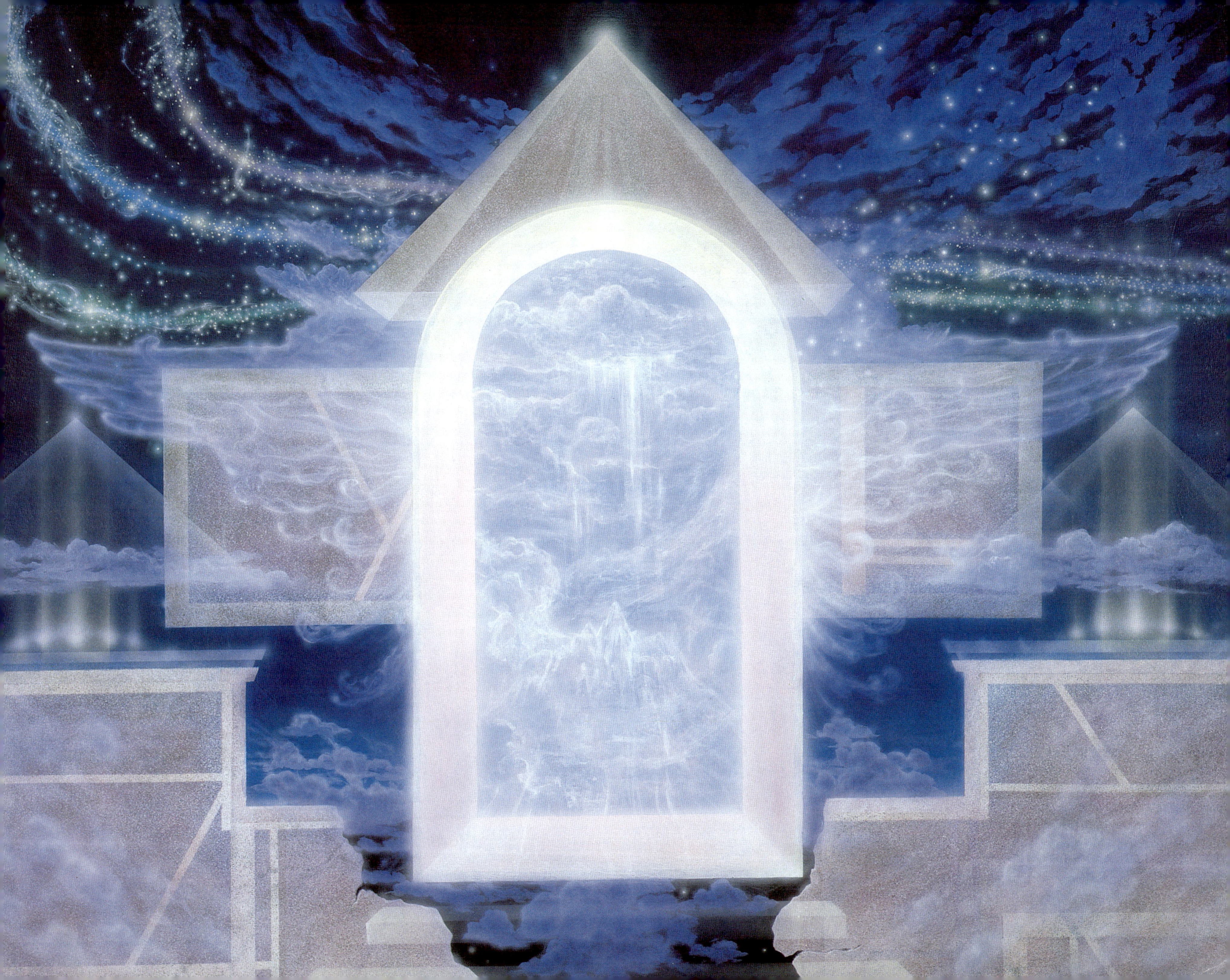

12. PORTAL OF THE PLEIADES

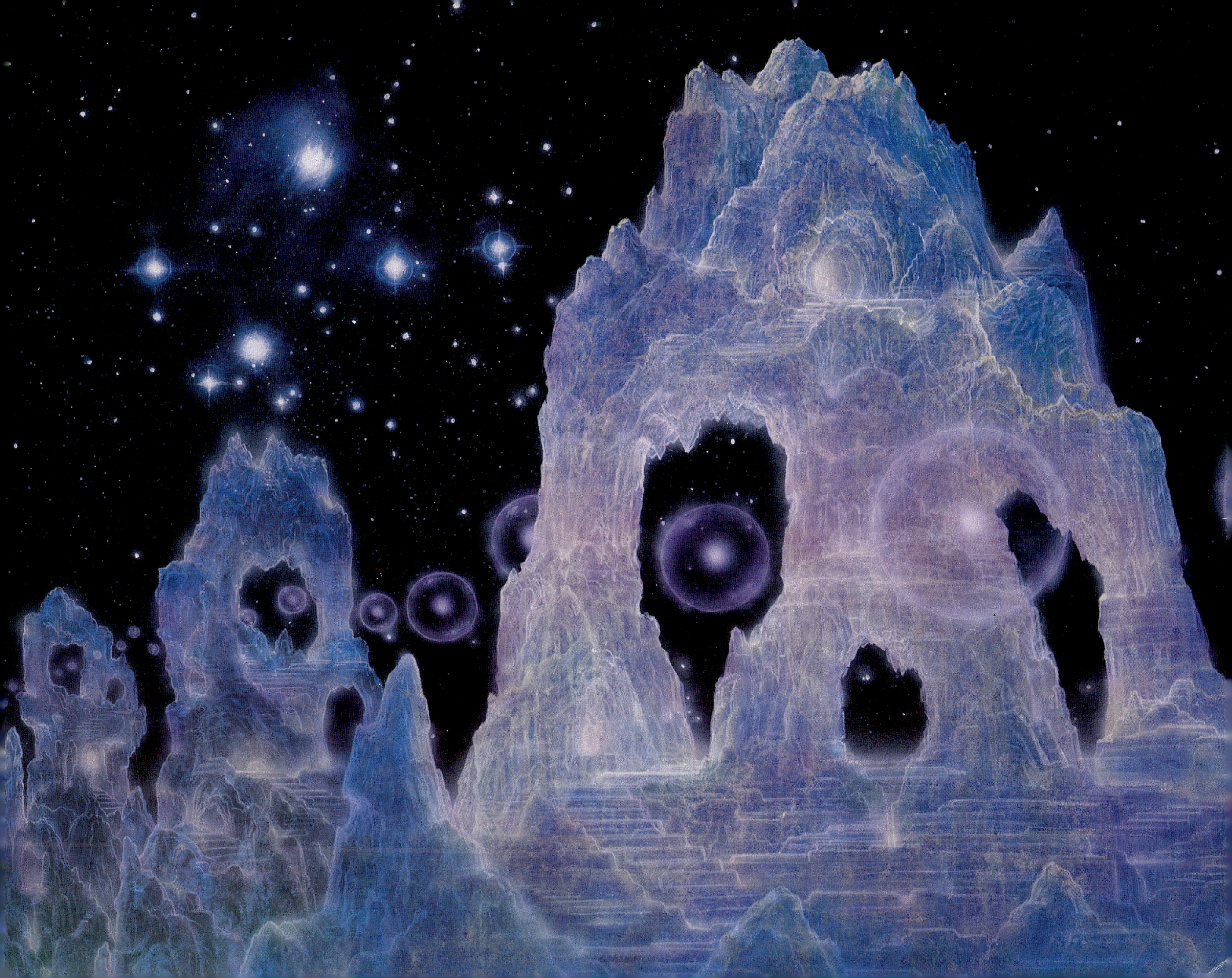

13. REFLECTION POOL

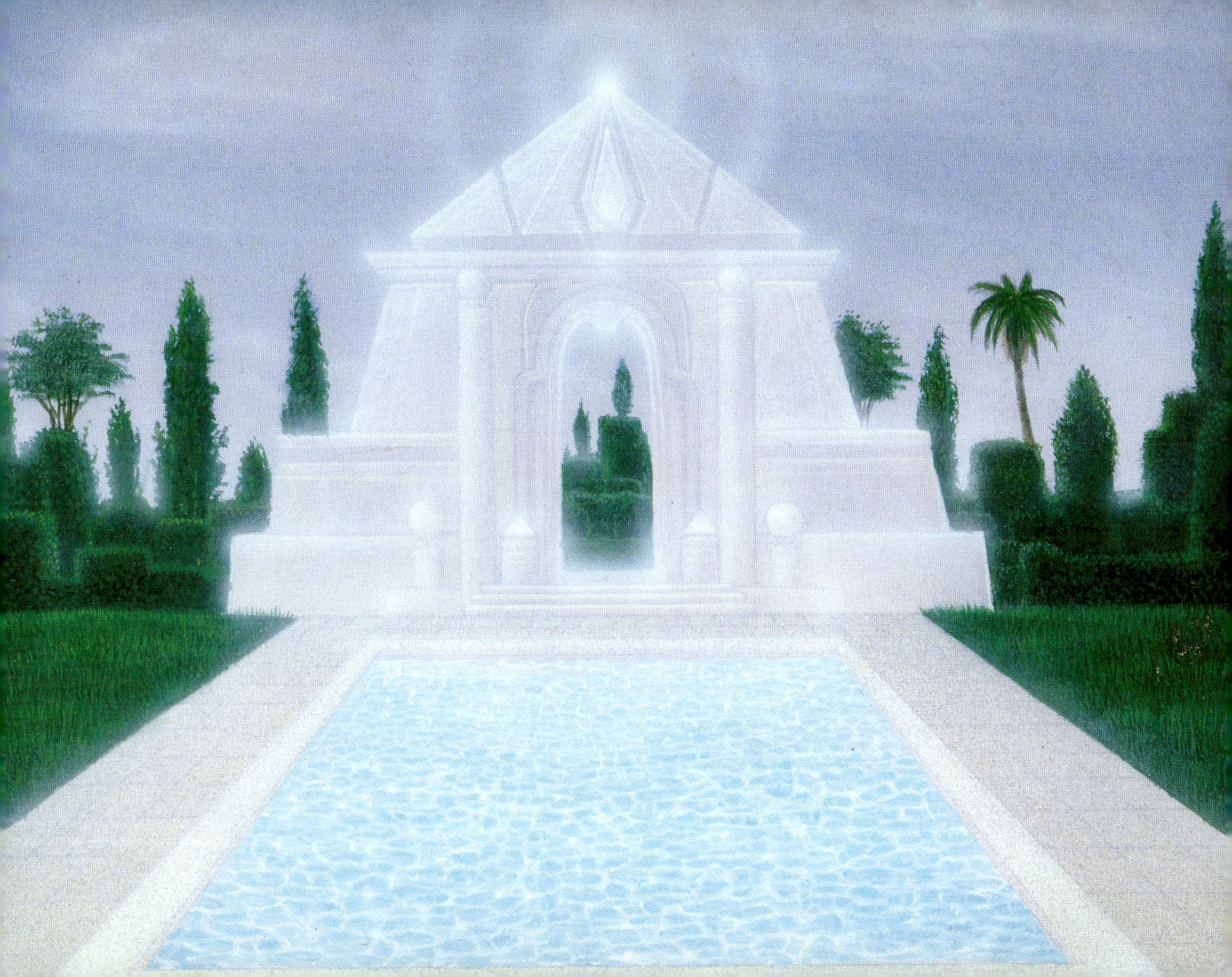

14. SACRED FOREST

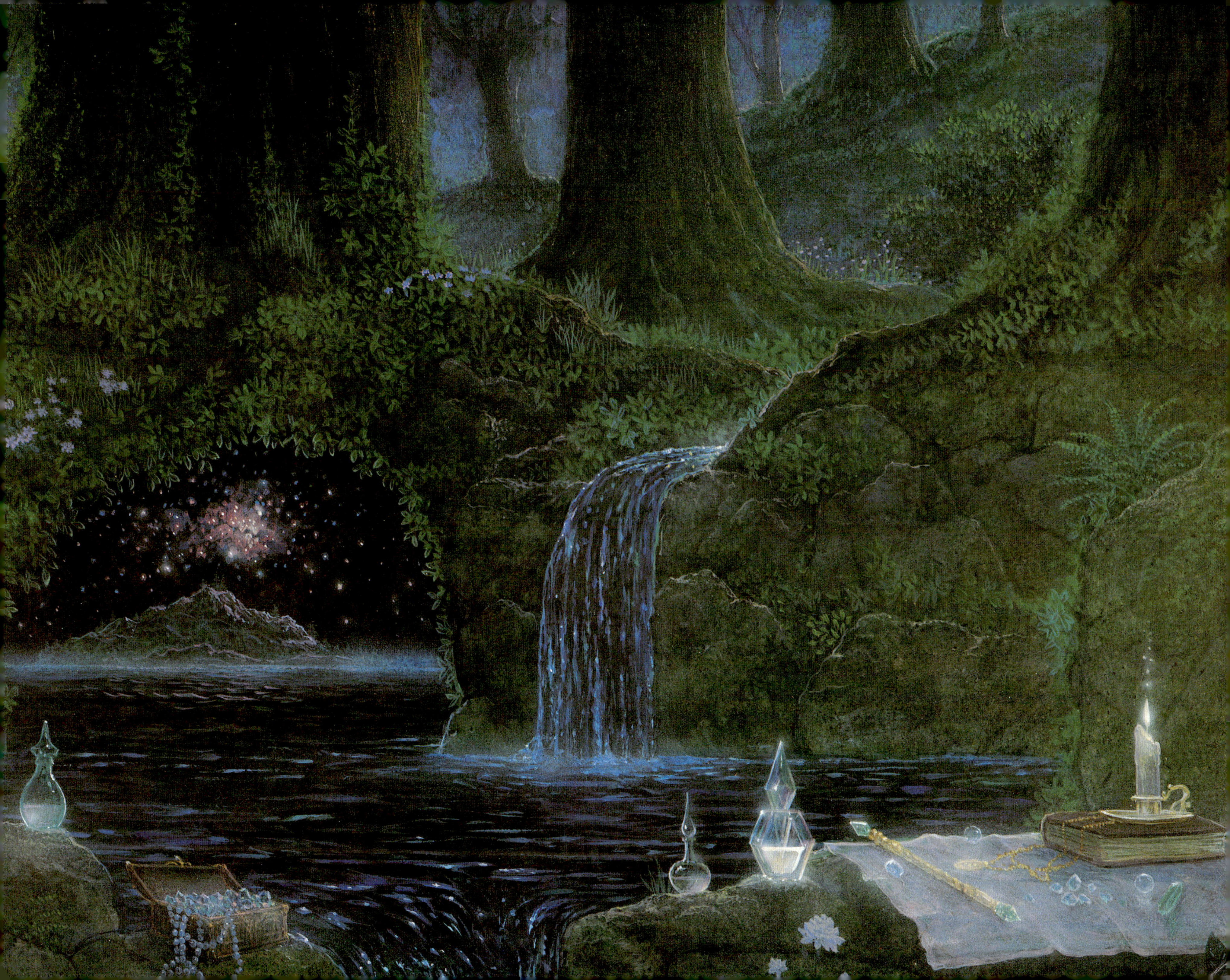

15. THE SHRINE

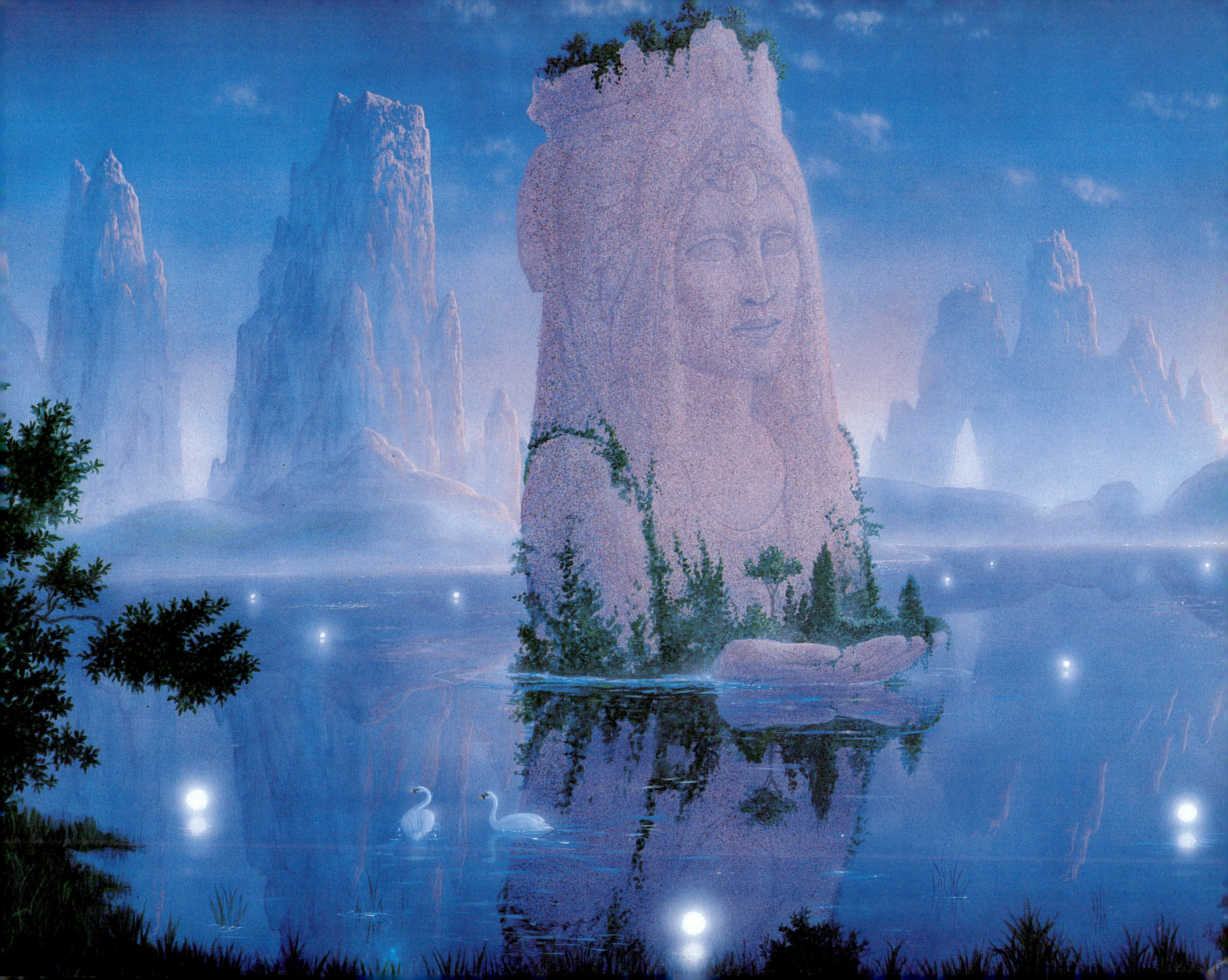

16. TREASURE SHIP

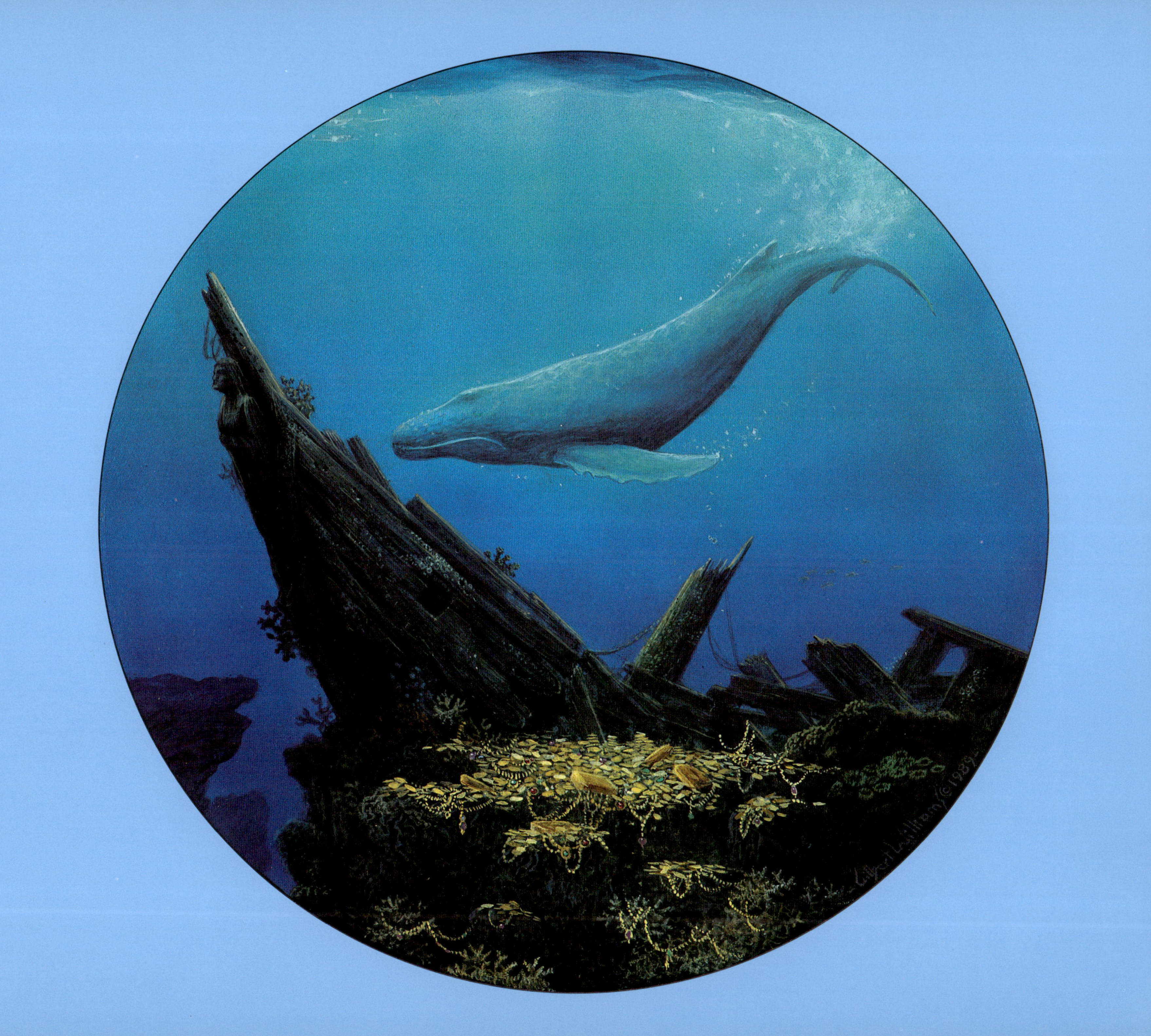

17. VISUALIZATION

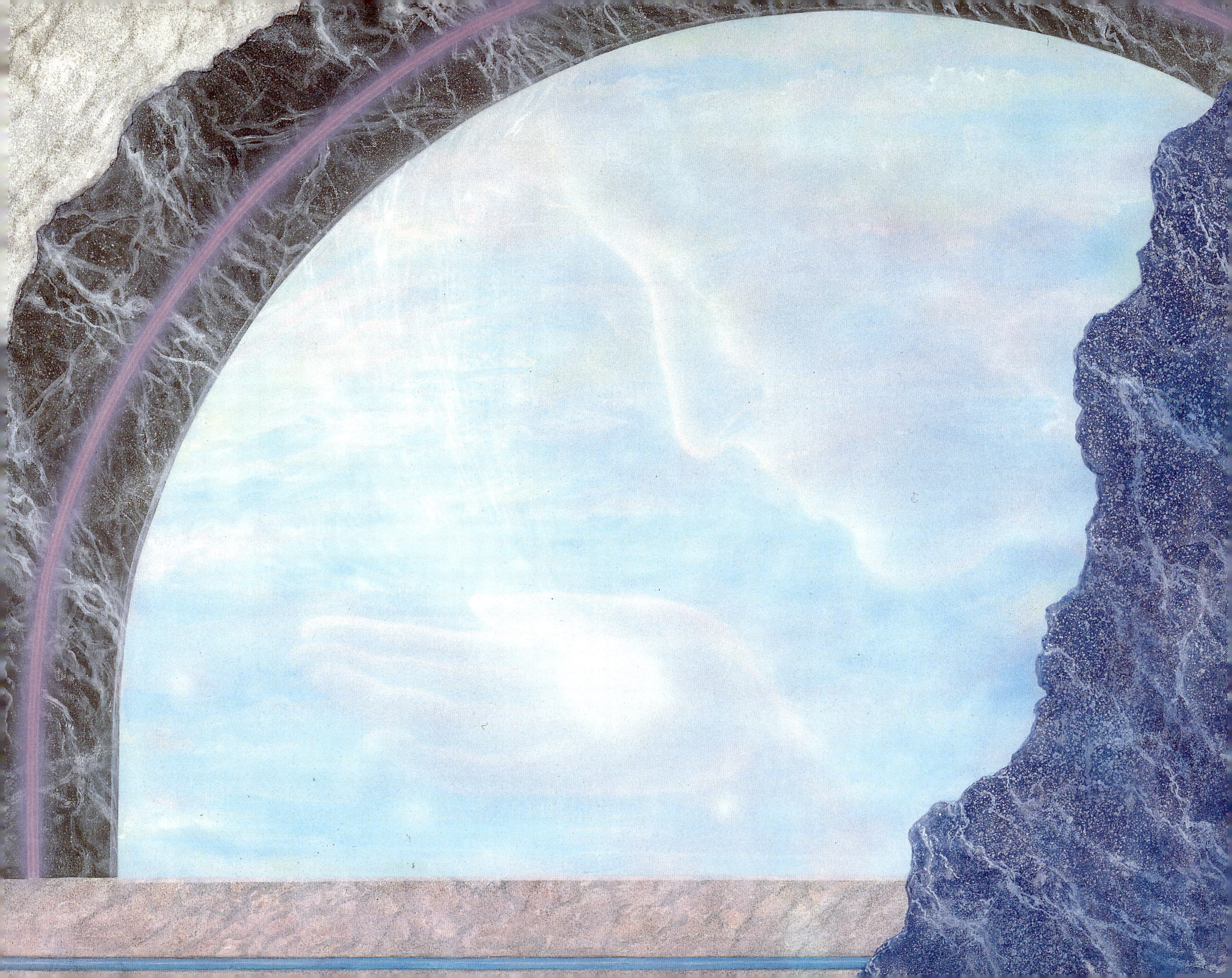

18. WISDOM

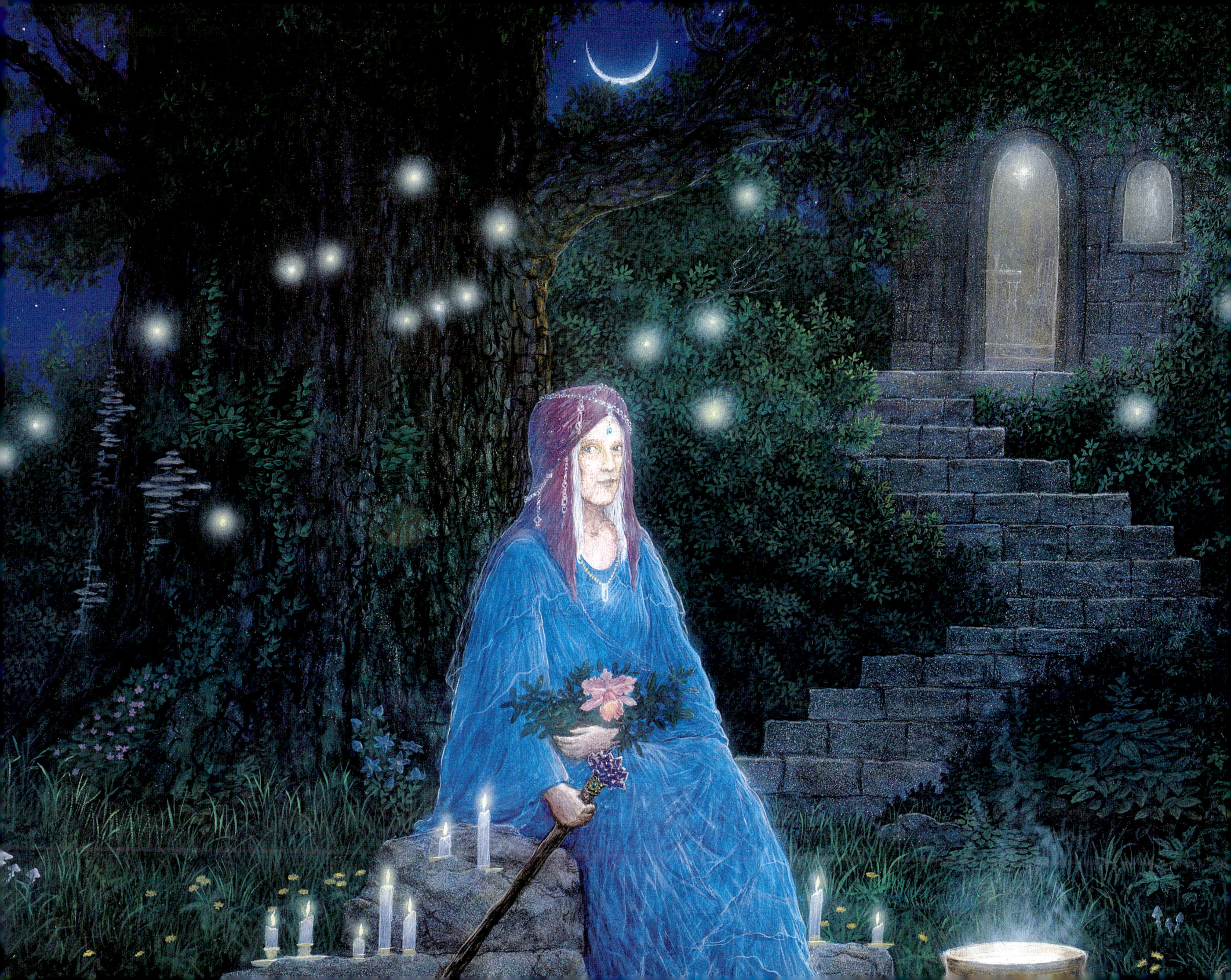

19. ABUNDANCE

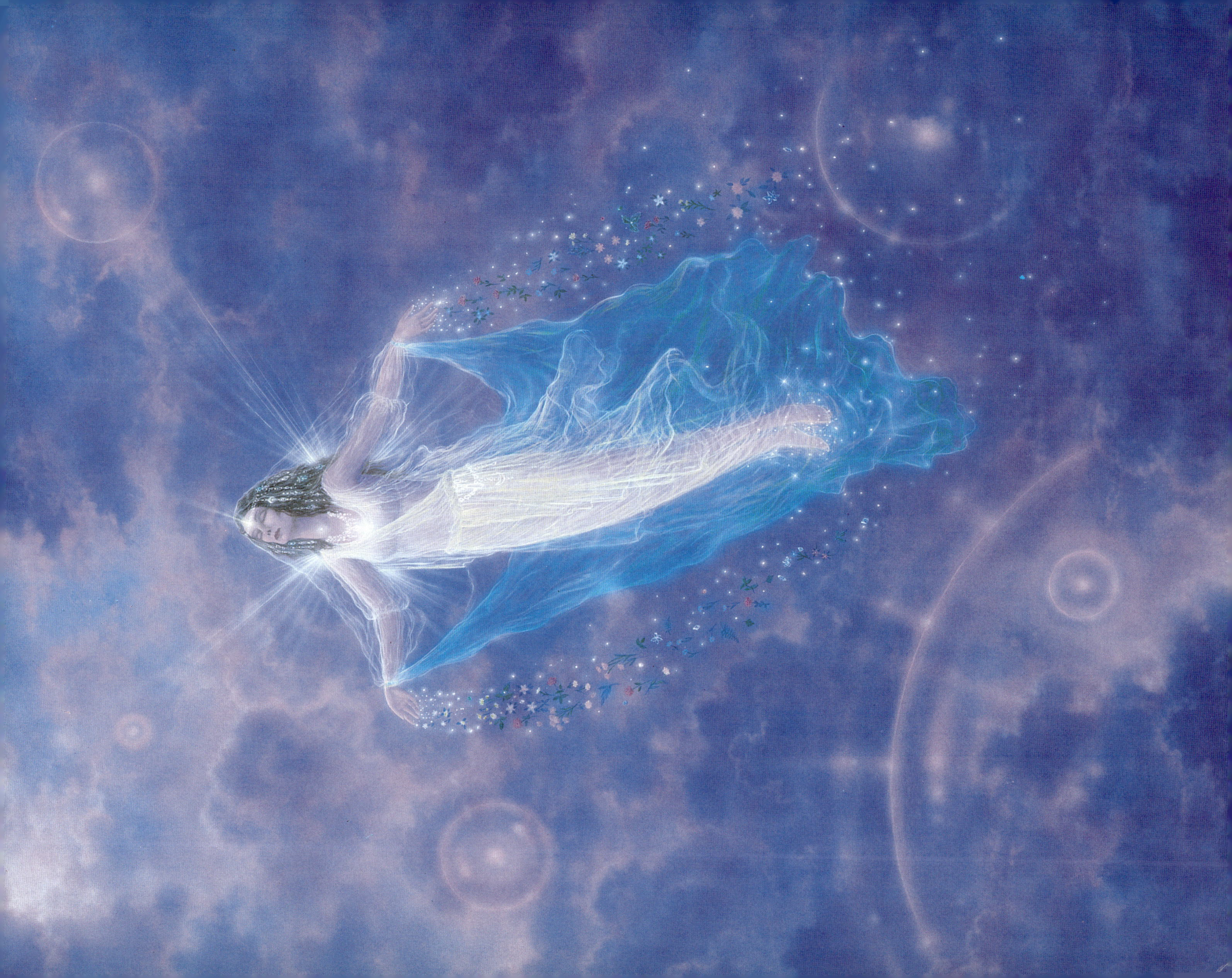

20. CLOUD SPIRIT

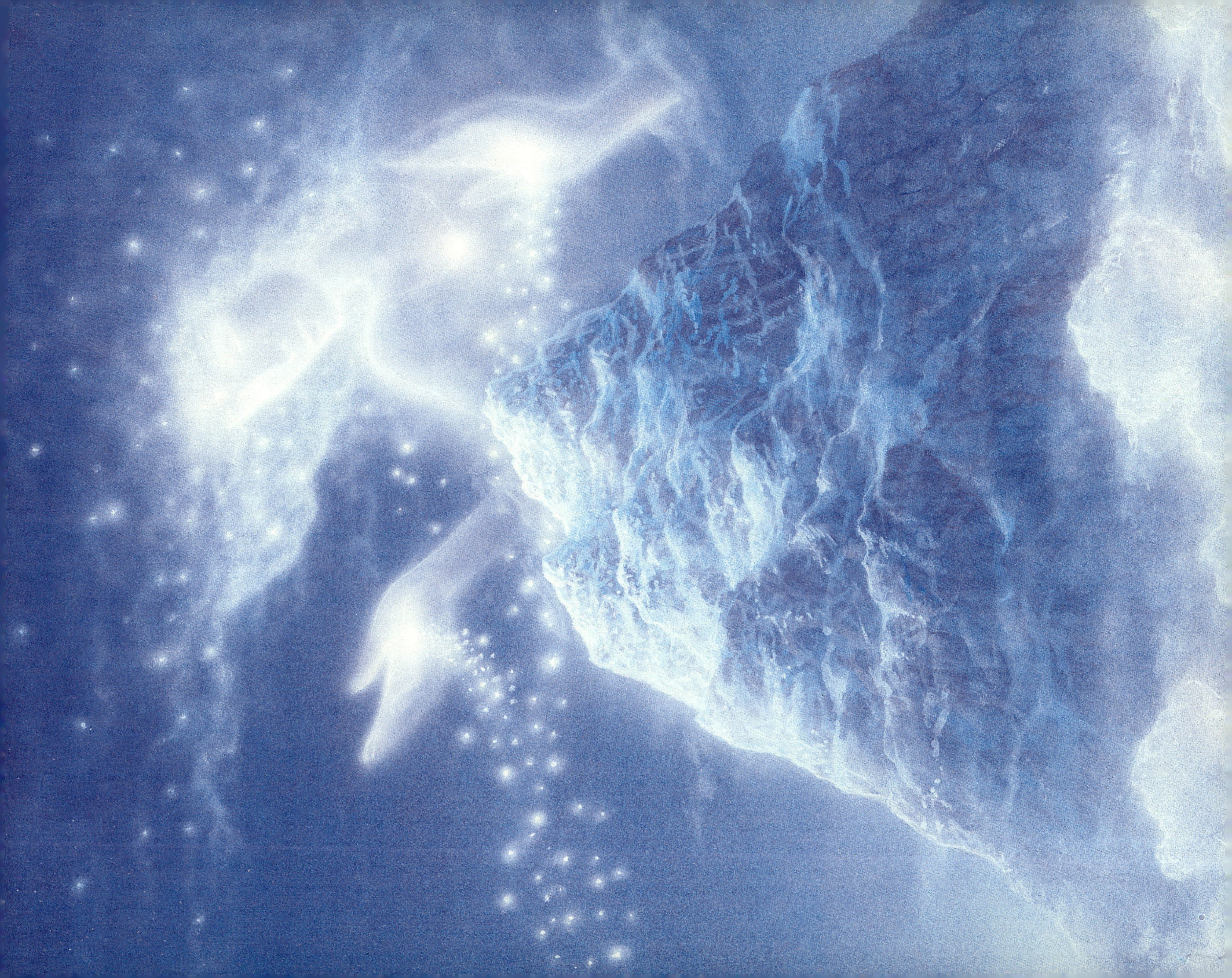

21. CRYSTAL FOUNTAIN

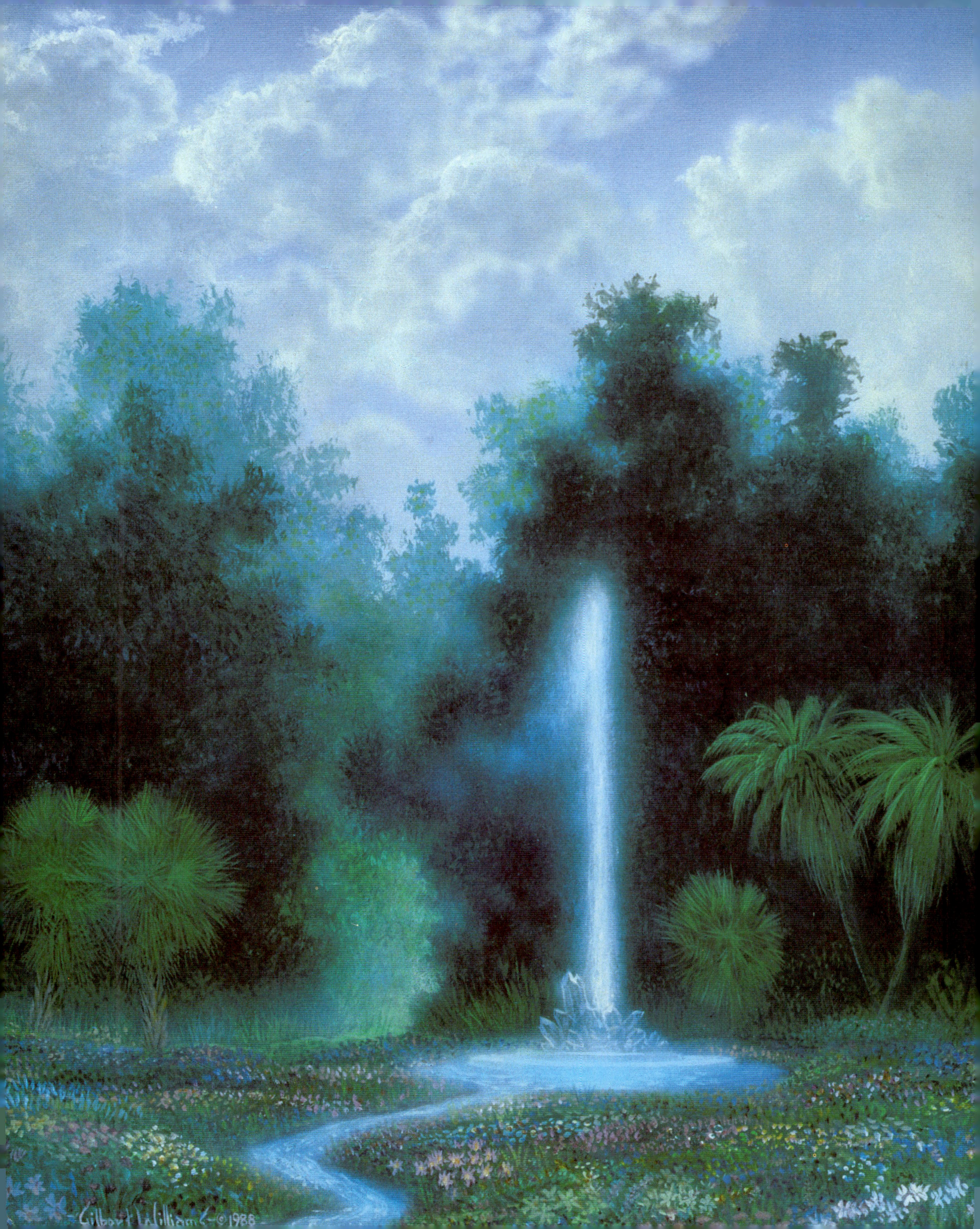
Gilbert Williams ©1988

22. DOLPHIN DAWN

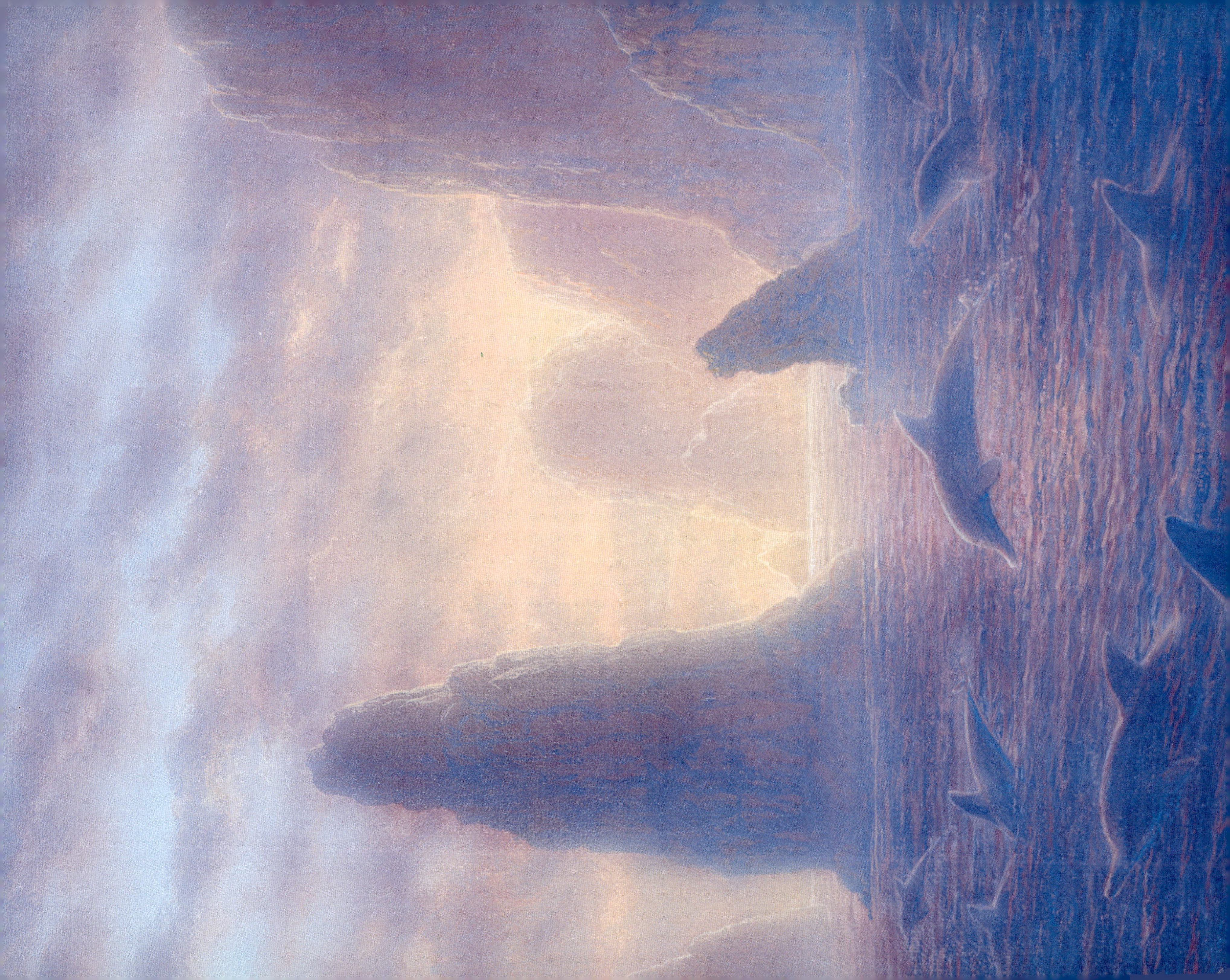

23. ENTRANCE INTO THE EARTH

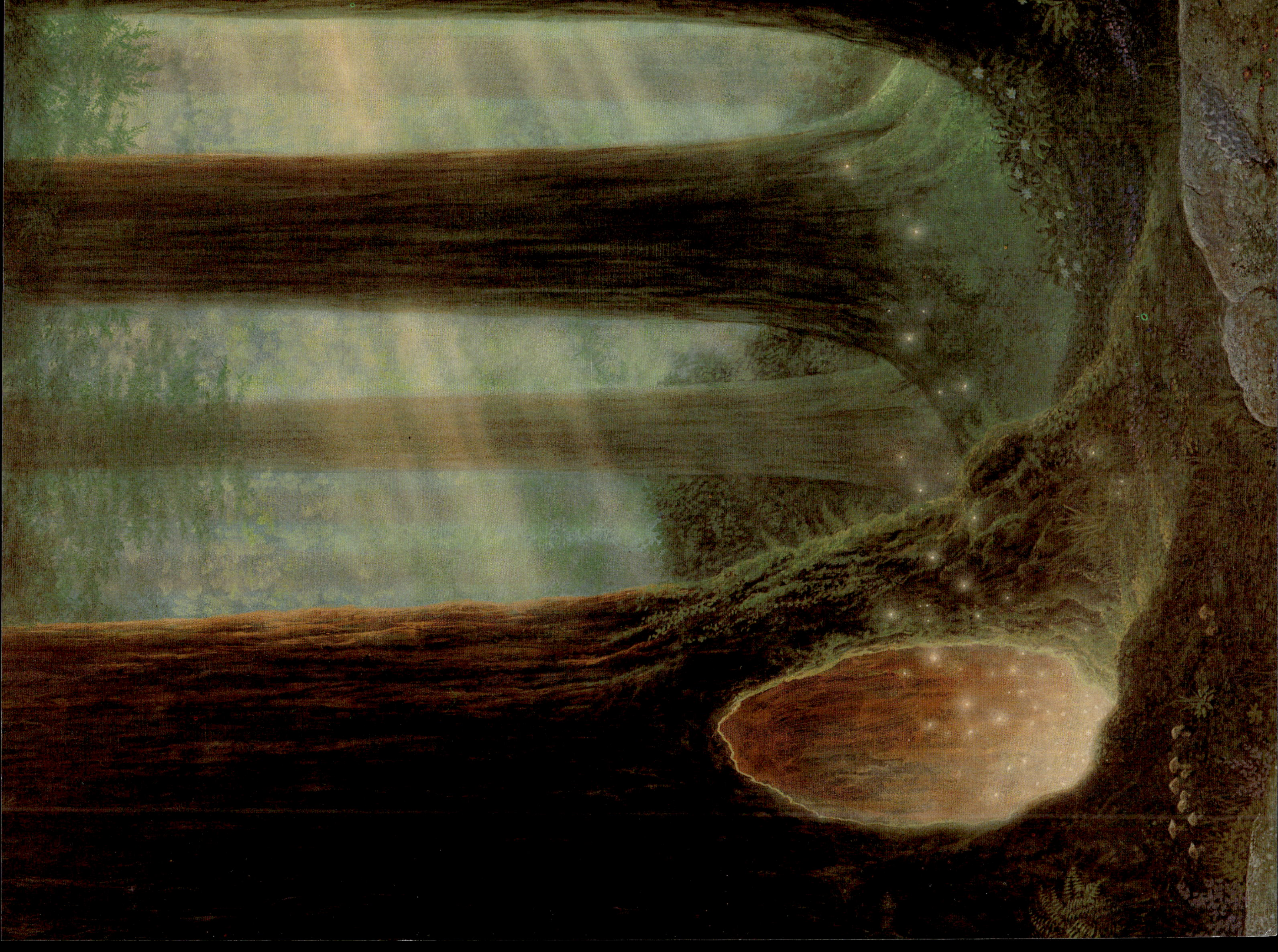

24. EXPLORERS

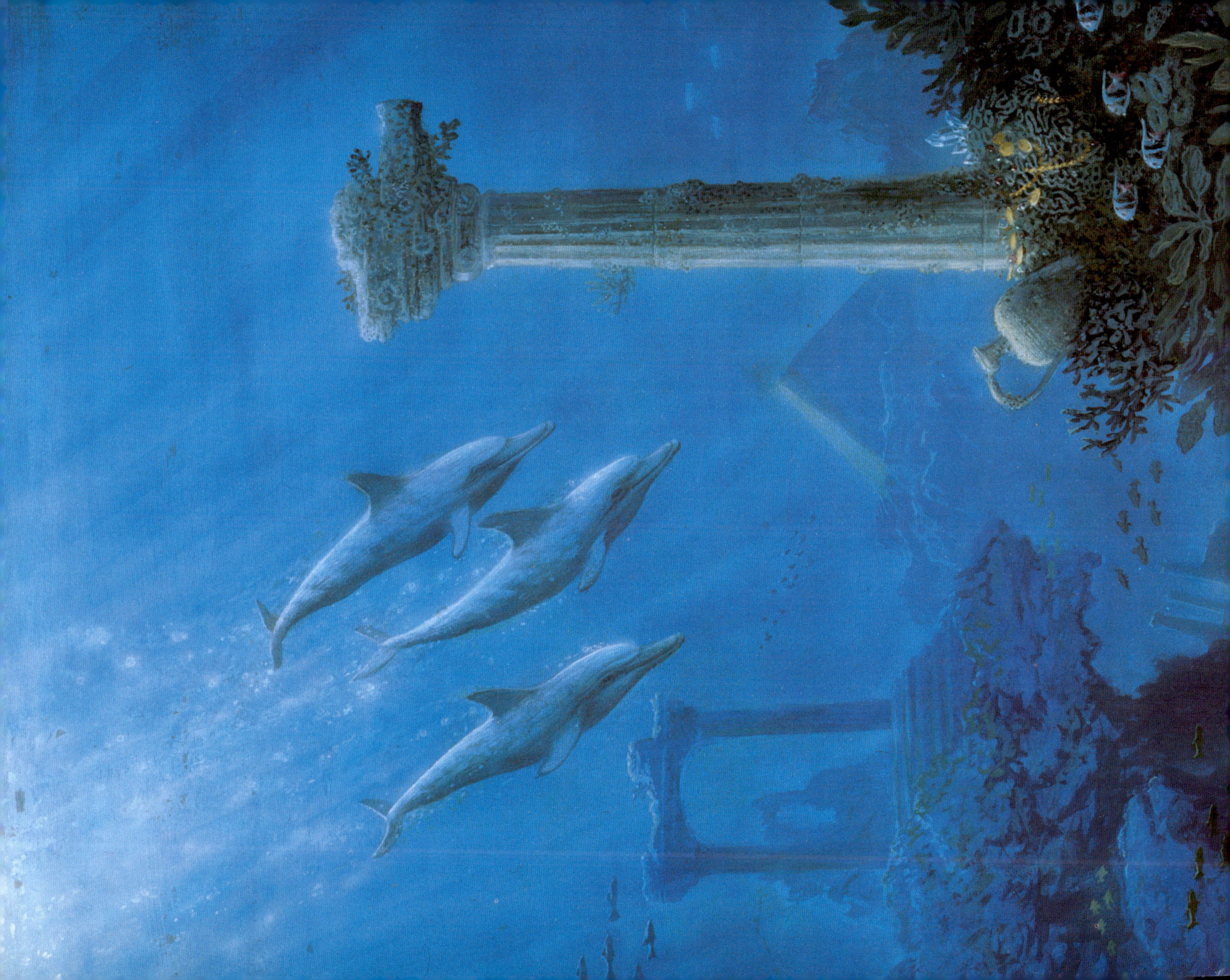

25. FAR HORIZONS

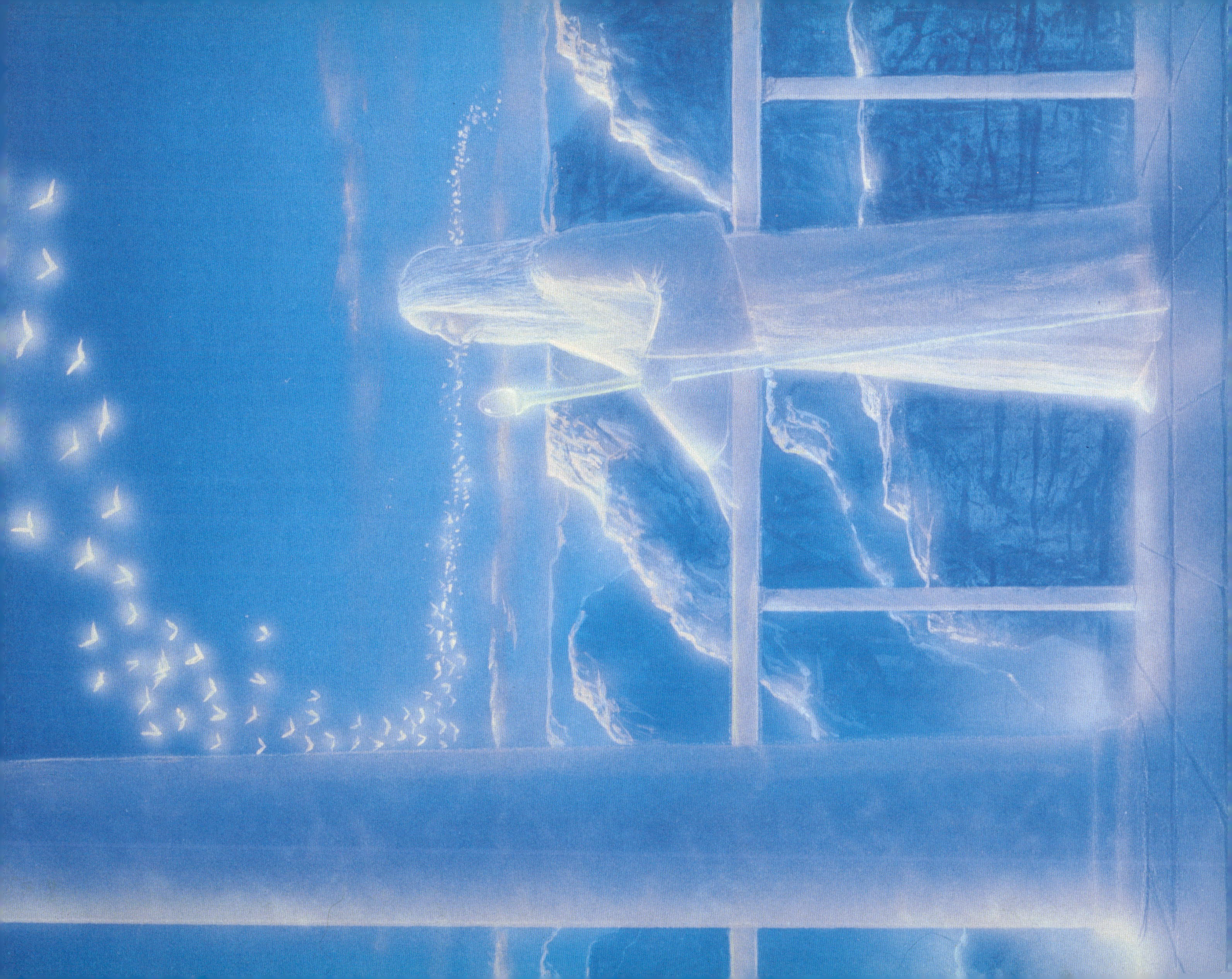

26. THE GATHERING

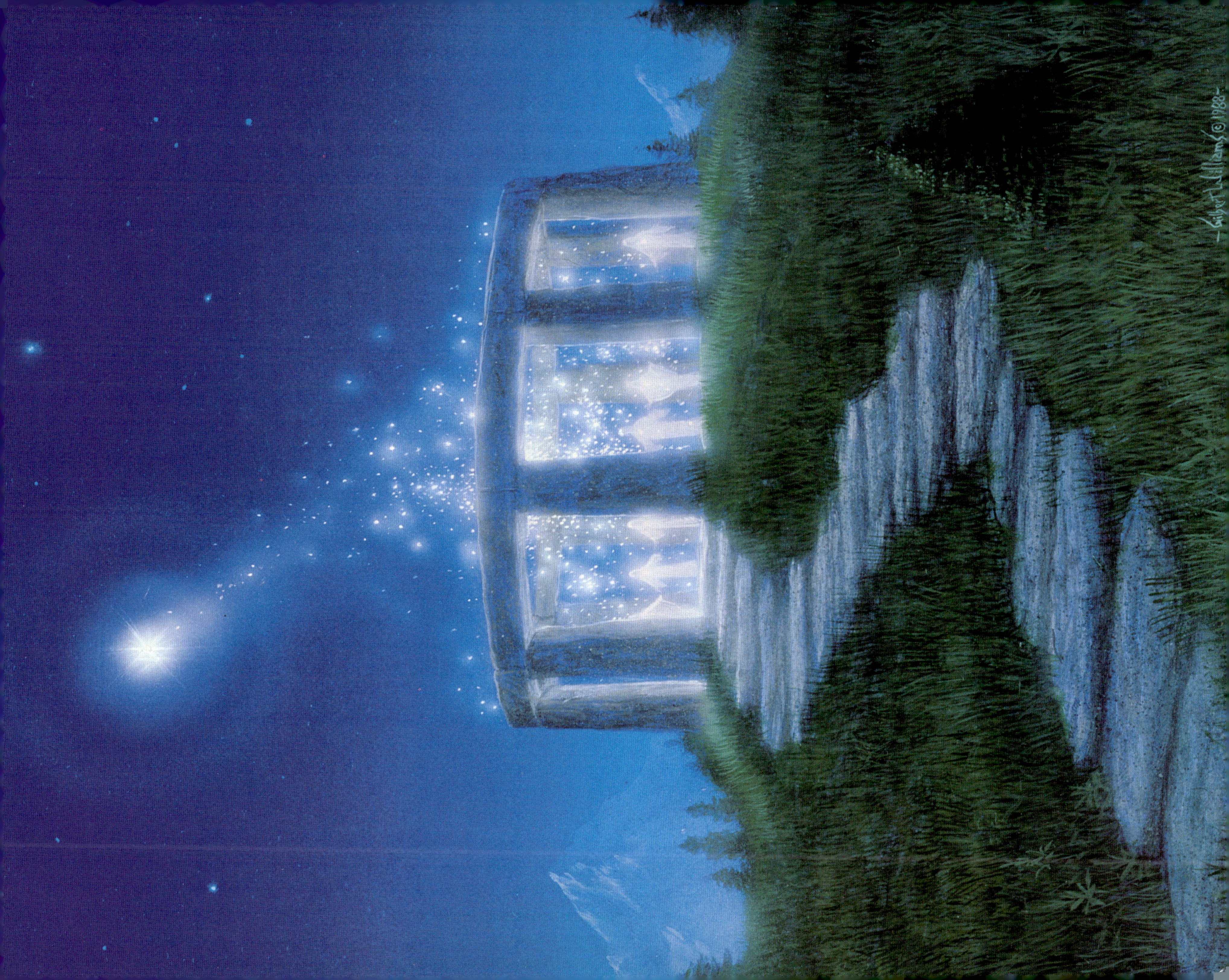

27. GATHERING FLOWERS

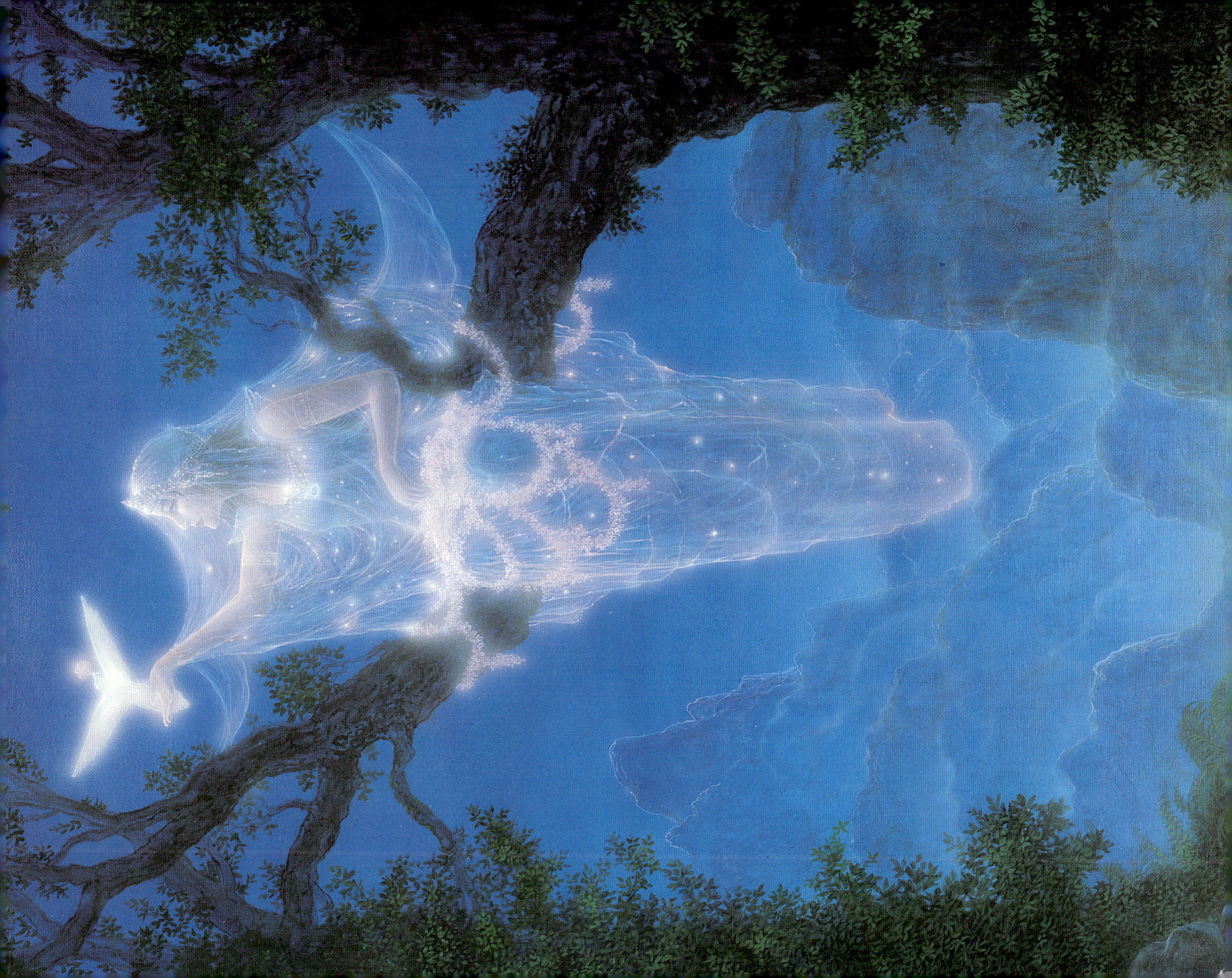

28. HIDDEN WORLDS

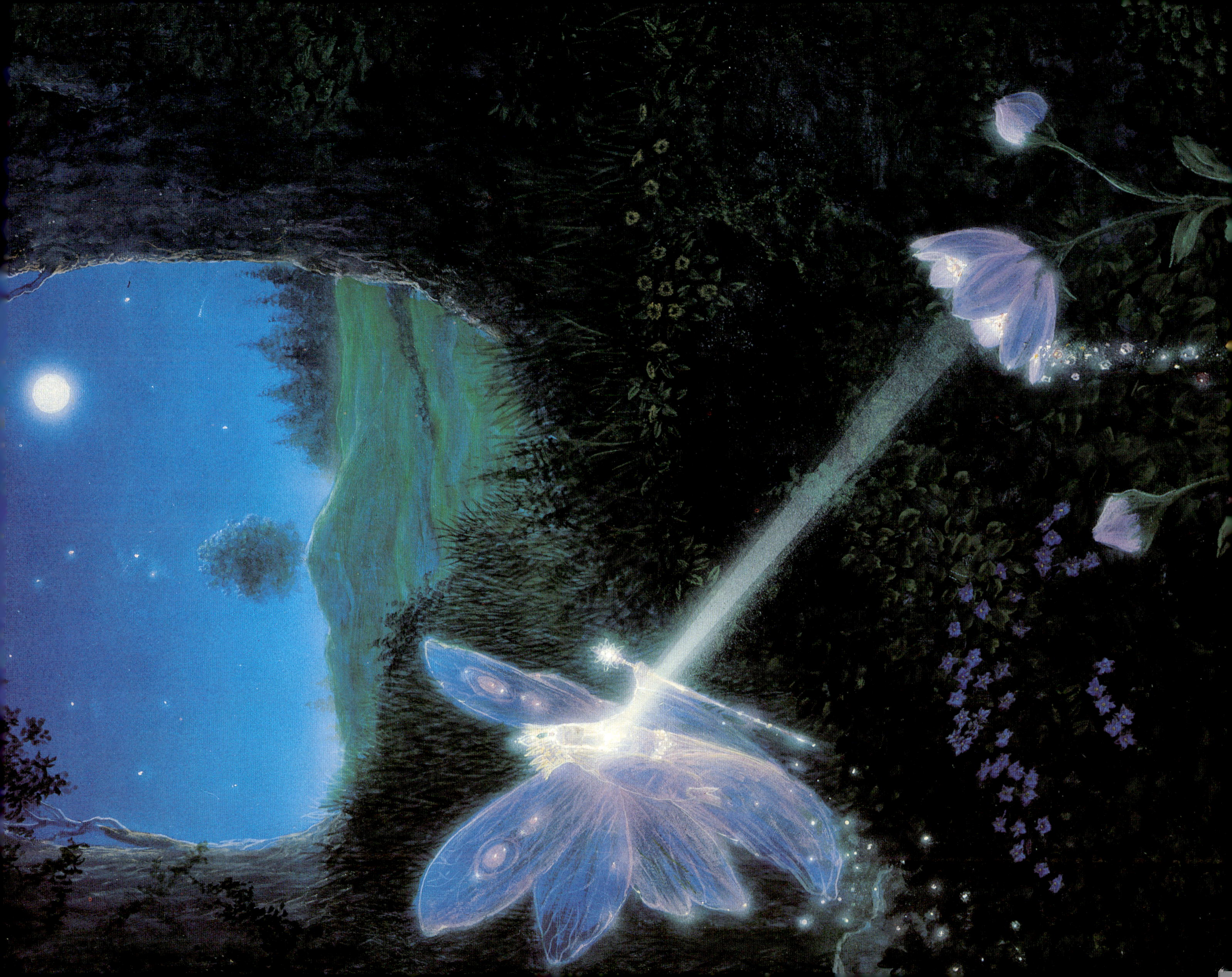

29. ILLUMINATION WINDOW

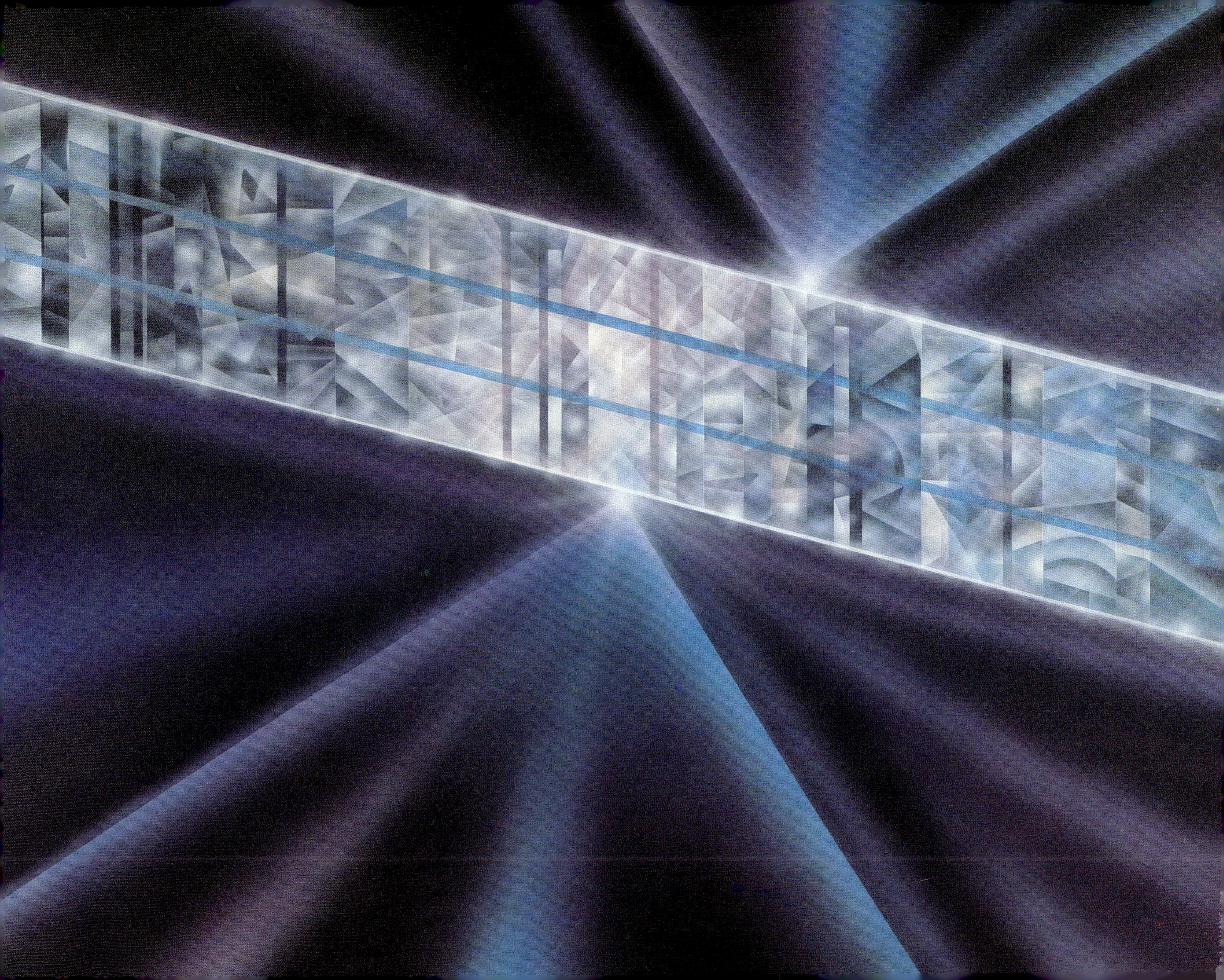

30. HOMEWARD TRAVELERS

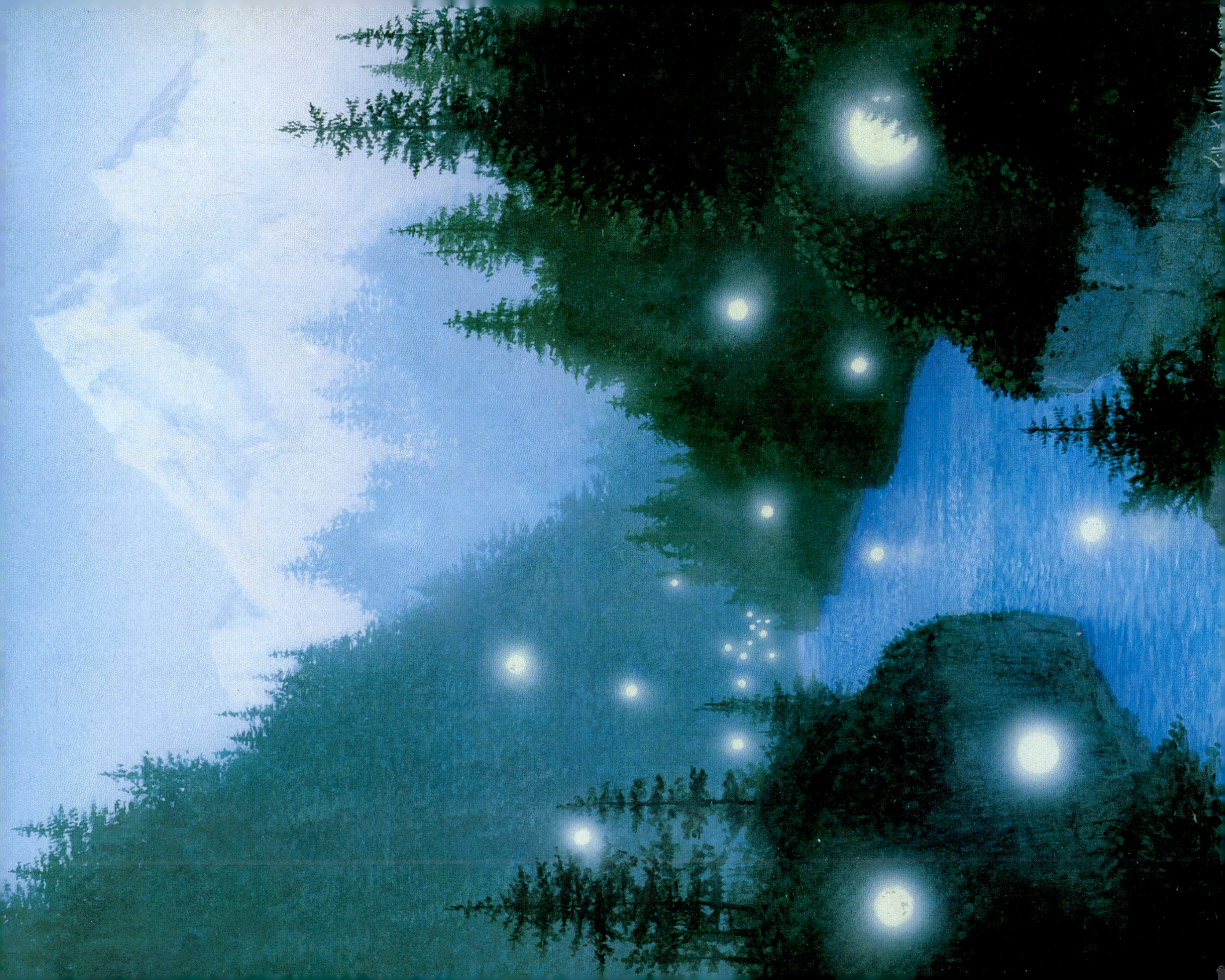

31. LADY OF THE LAKE

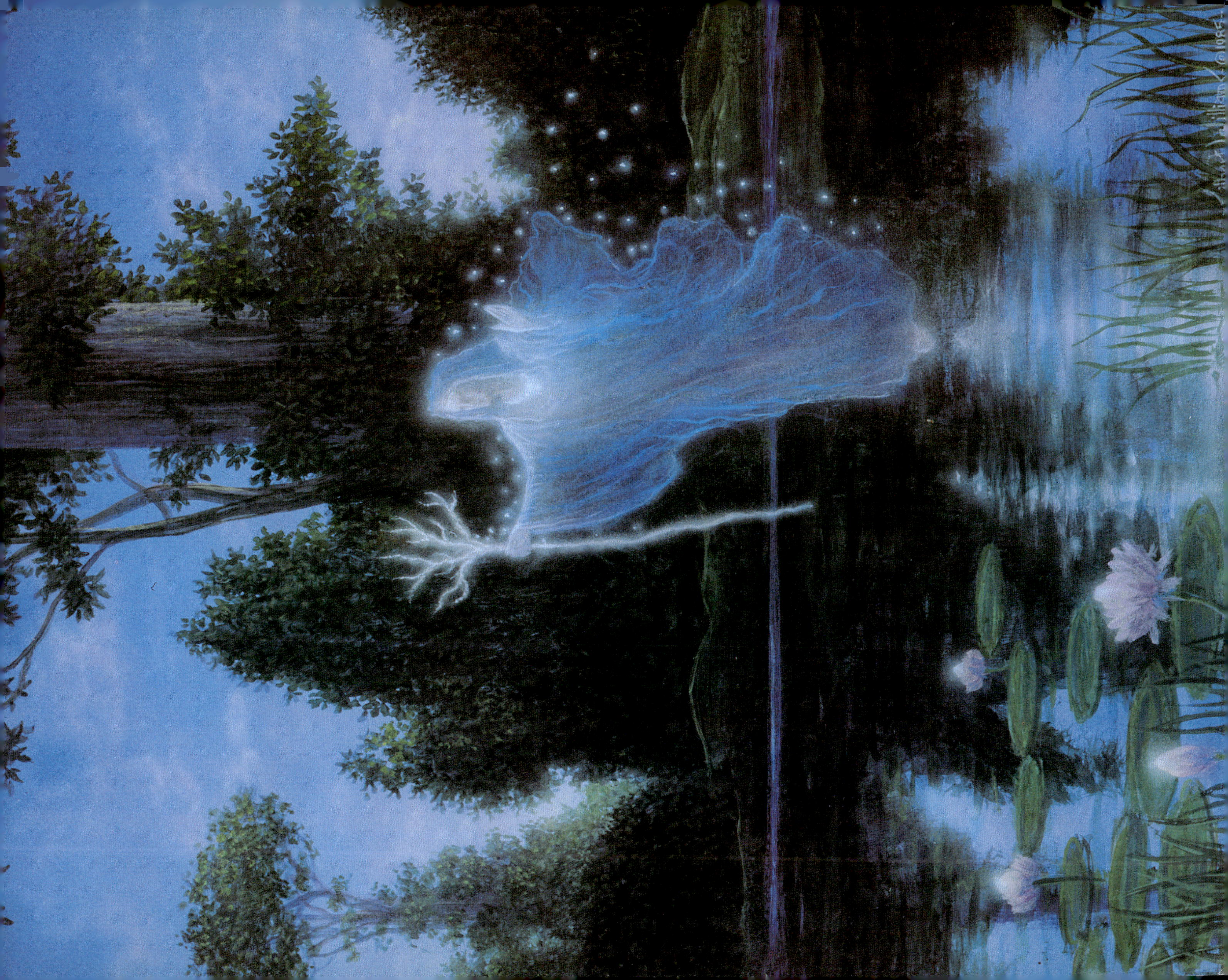

32. LAZARIS REMEMBERS LEMURIA

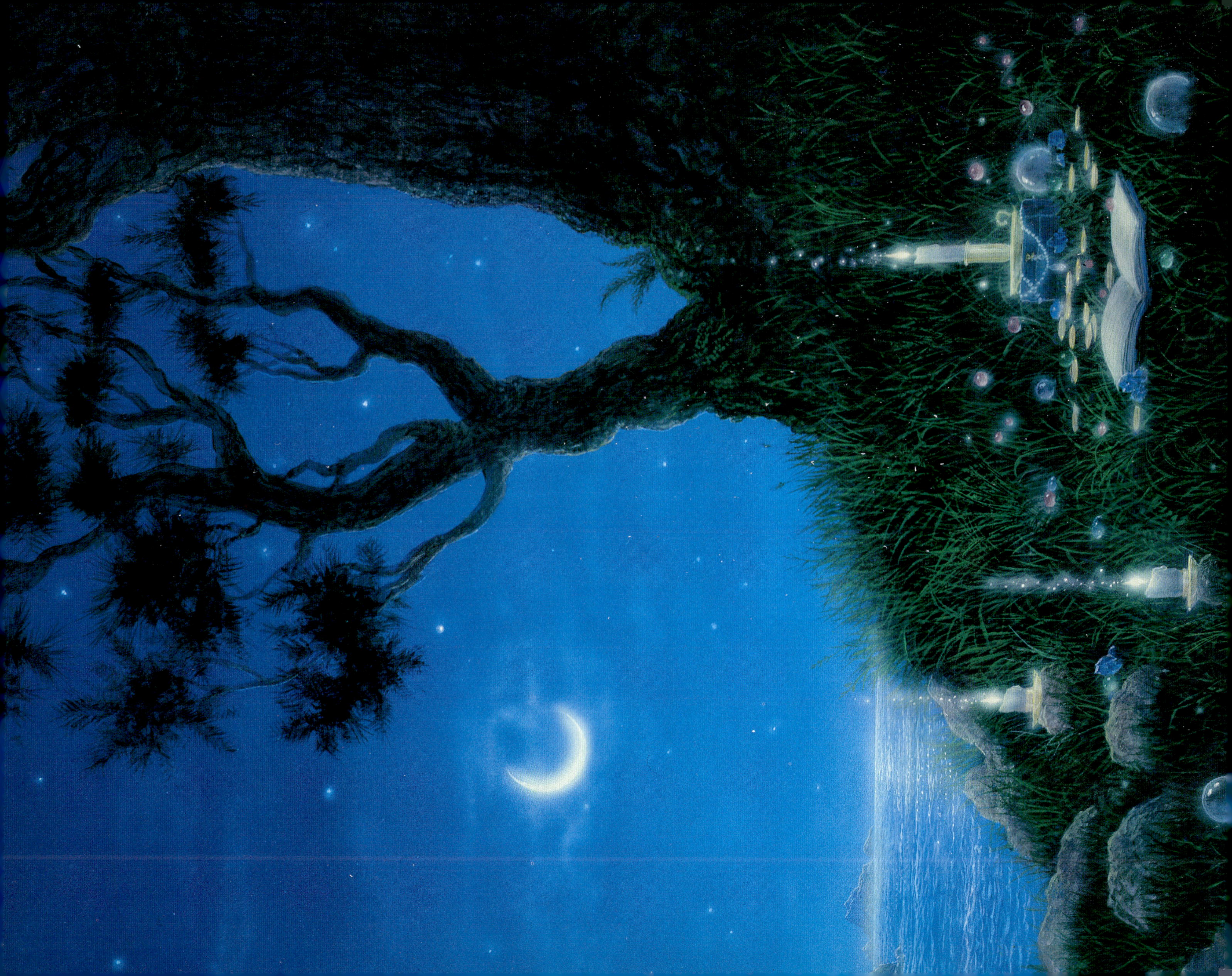

33. MIST ANGEL

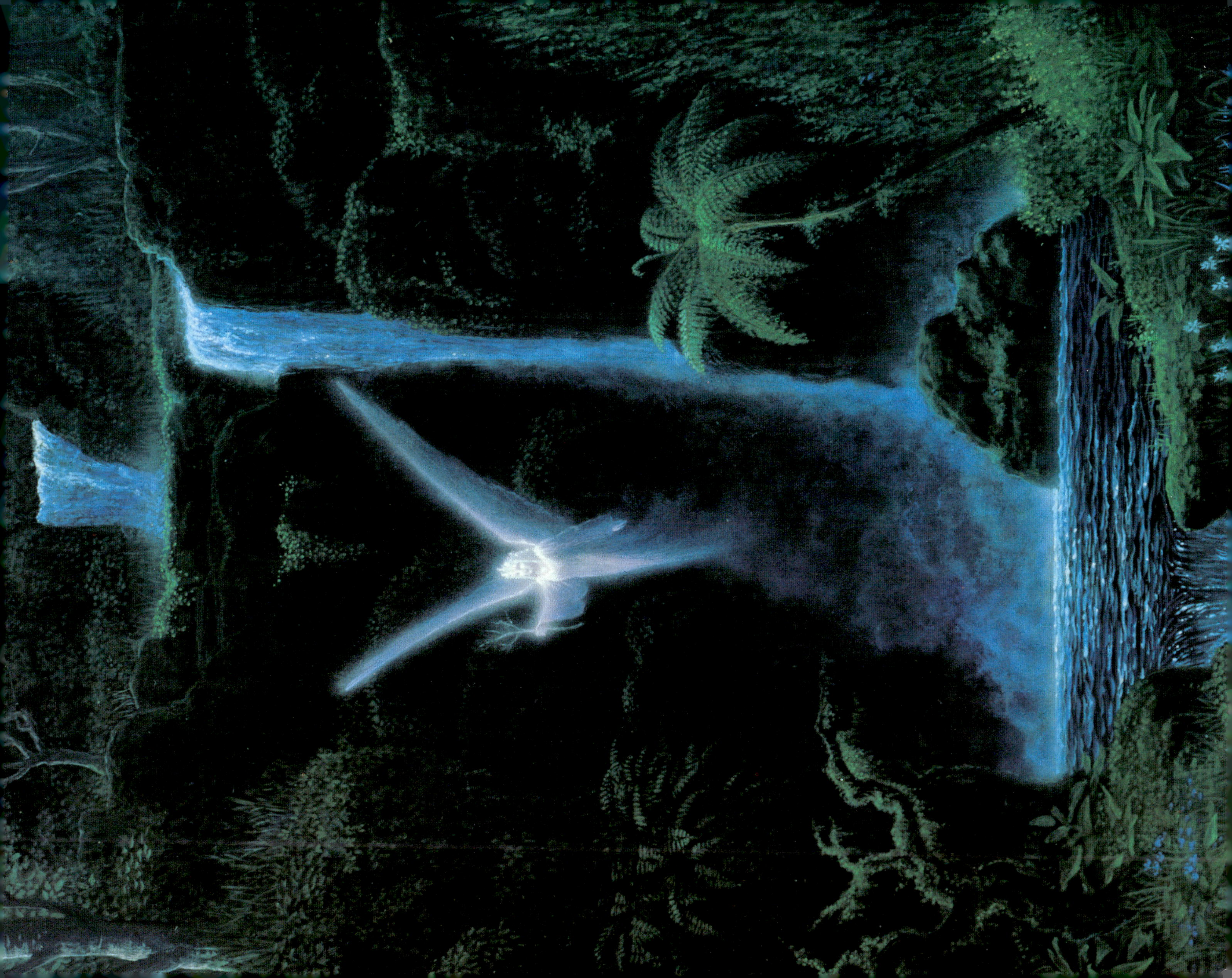

34. SACRED JOURNEY

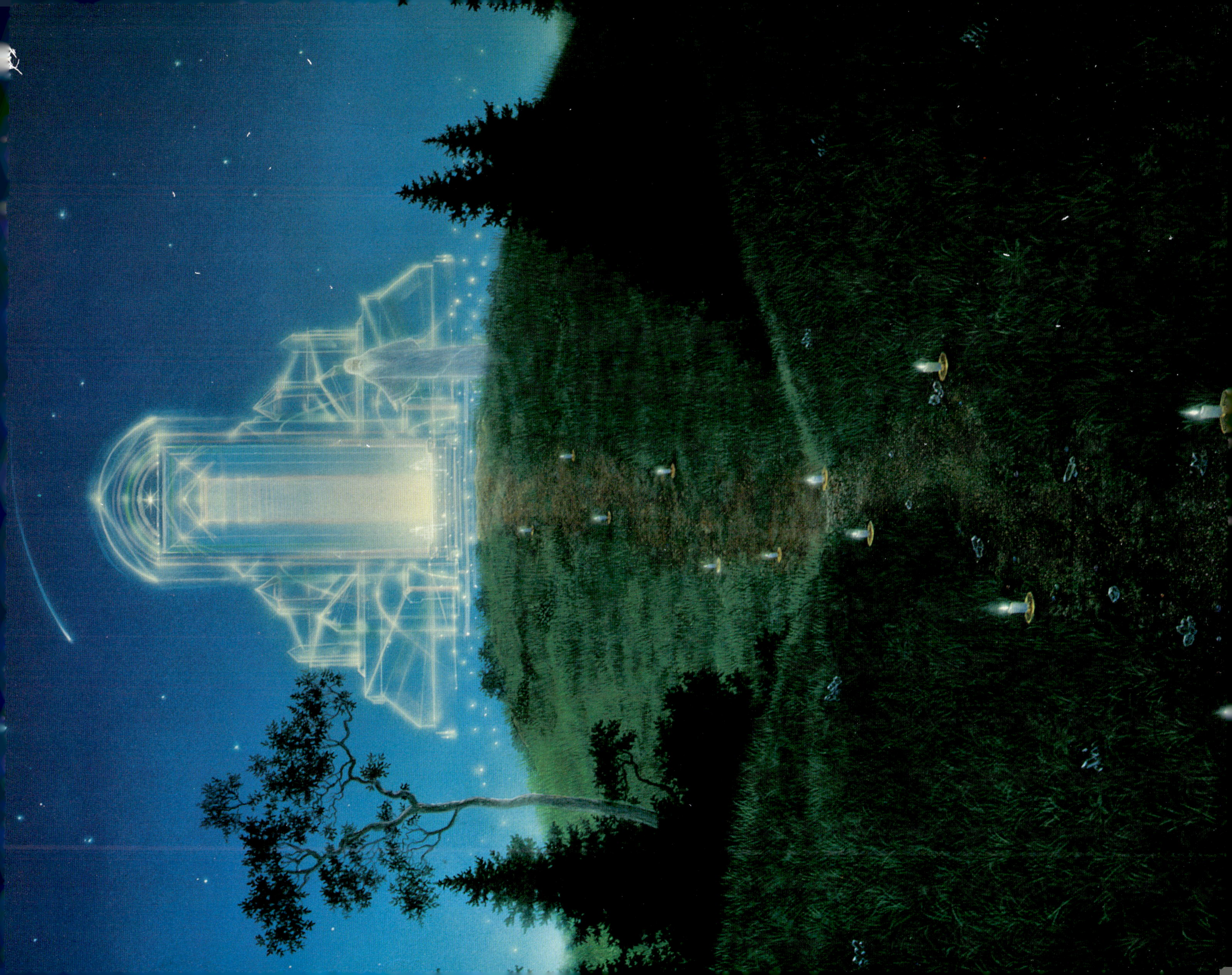

35. TROUBADOUR OF SPRING

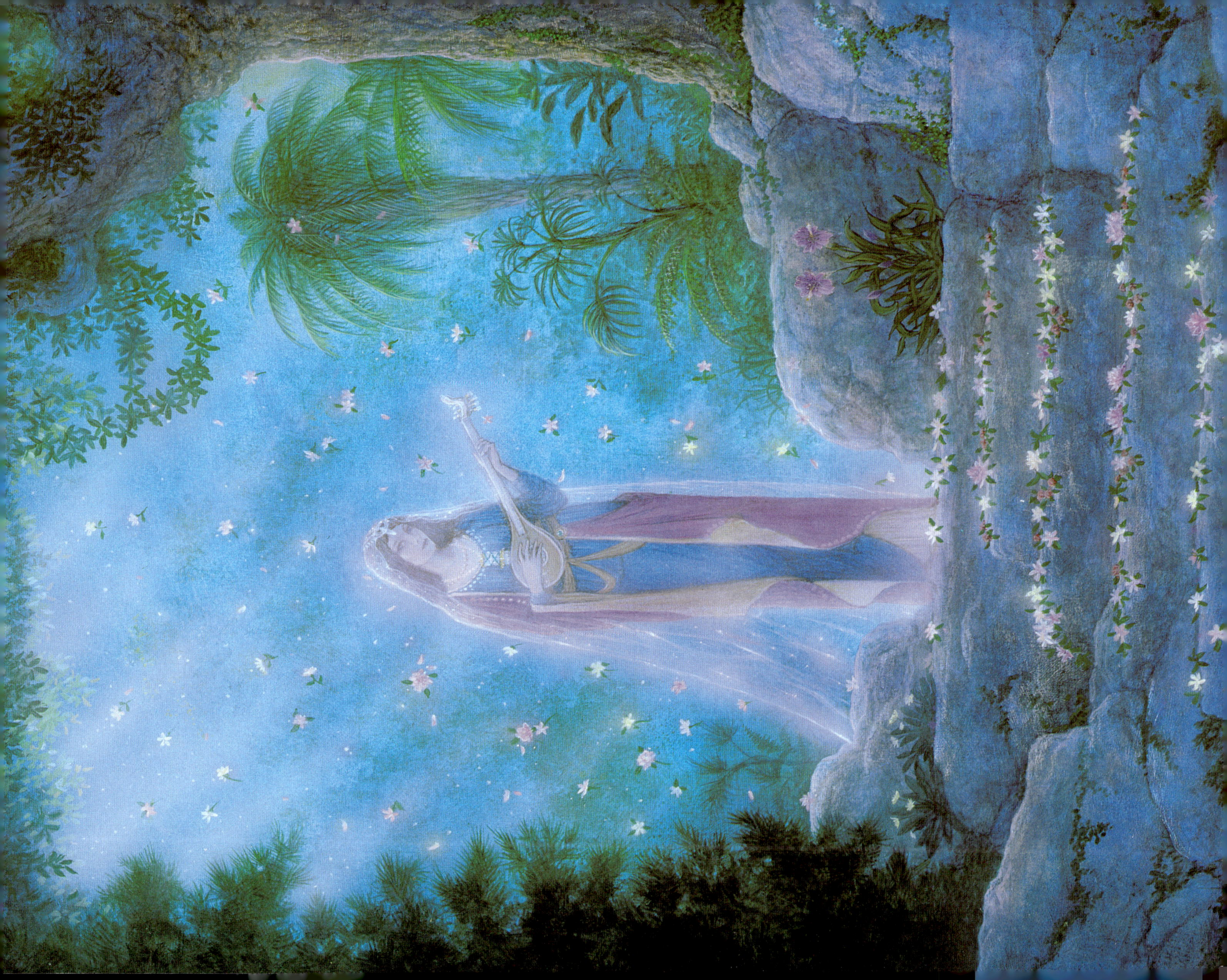

36. THE WAY SHOWER

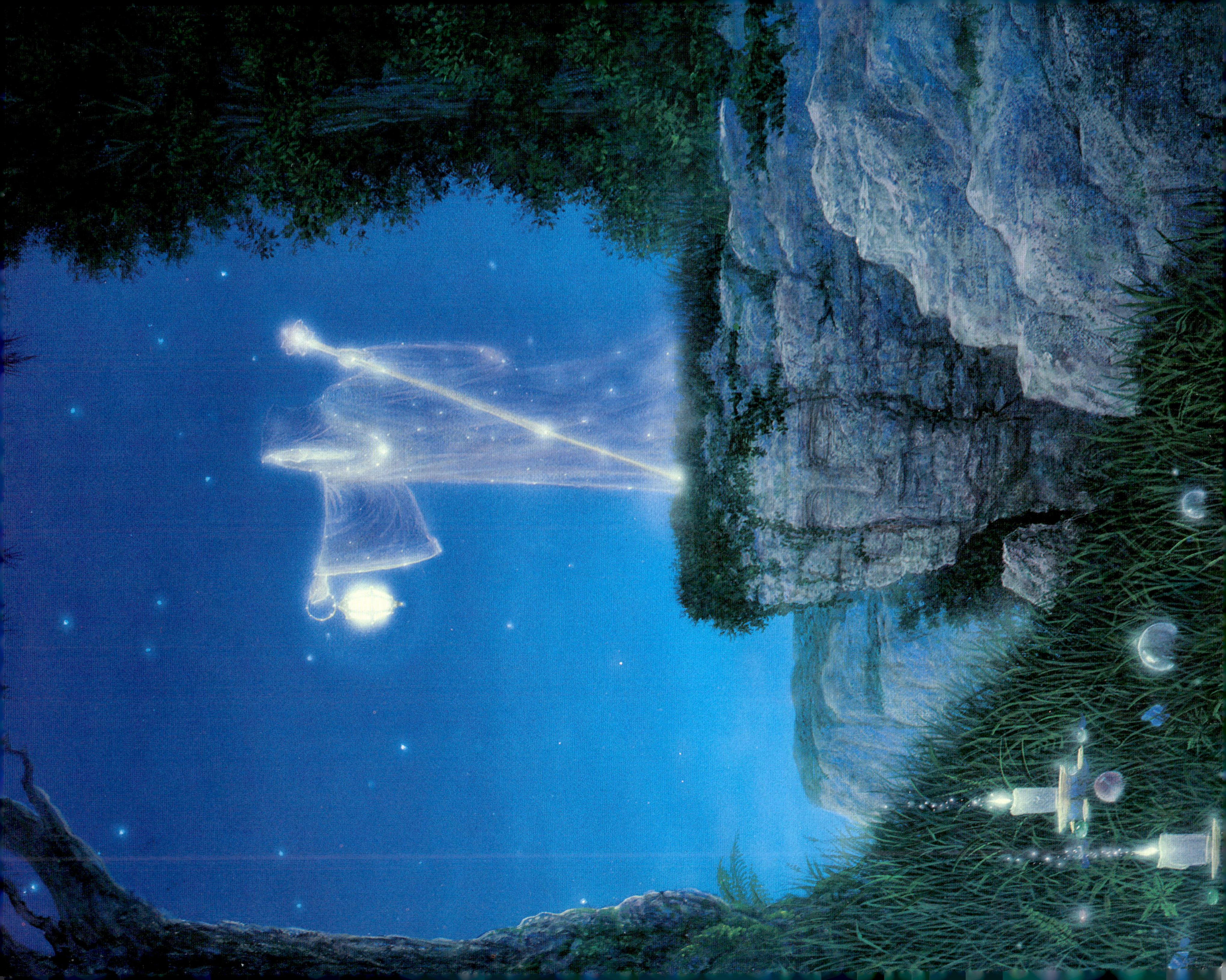

Isis Rising

Exclusive Agent for Original Paintings and Lithographs by Gilbert Williams

Isis Rising, created from the merger of Isis Unlimited and Illuminarium Gallery, Inc., is the exclusive agent for originals by Gilbert Williams, other accomplished contemporary painters, and some of the finest sculptors, ceramicists, glass artists, and jewelry artists in the world. Isis Rising also carries an expansive collection of rare natural crystals from Madagascar and Brazil as well as extraordinary collectible dolls.

Isis Rising is located at The Galleria at Fort Lauderdale
2398(A) East Sunrise Boulevard, E-15 (next to Neiman Marcus)
Fort Lauderdale, Florida 33304
305/566-8088

Visionary Publishing, Inc.

Notecards, Calendars, and Art Books by Gilbert Williams and Other Fine Visionary Painters

Visionary Publishing, Inc., winner of a 1989 Award of Merit for design and printing from the Printing Industries of America, publishes many of Gilbert Williams' finest images as notecards, as well as many by other Visionary painters. Each year Visionary Publishing also prints the exquisitely beautiful ***Lazaris - Gilbert Williams Calendar***, a calendar of 12 images by Gilbert Williams with empowering and remarkably helpful quotes by Lazaris for each month. Visionary Publishing also publishes other calendars, and the two Gilbert Williams art books:
Illuminations: The Visionary Art of Gilbert Williams (Volume I) and
The Hidden Worlds: The Visionary Art of Gilbert Williams, Volume II
Other art books by Gilbert Williams are forthcoming from Visionary Publishing.

For a Catalog from Visionary Publishing, Inc.

To receive a Visionary Publishing catalog, please send $1.00 in check or money order to: Visionary Publishing, Inc., 302 South County Road, Suite 230, Palm Beach, FL 33480. We will then send you a catalog sheet of all our notecards, calendars, and books — and a coupon for $1.00 which is redeemable with any order of $10.00 or more.